Governing a Poor Country

Perspectives from a Former Chief Minister of Sierra Leone

Professor Ruard Ganzevoort
Rector - ISS, The Hague
With Best Wishes
J Francis
23/03/2026
'Alumni 1995'

Governing a Poor Country

Perspectives from a Former Chief Minister of Sierra Leone

David J. Francis

Governing a Poor Country

Perspectives from a Former Chief Minister of Sierra Leone

David J. Francis

Table of Contents

How to run a country? This is the challenge faced by political and economic leaders entrusted with running the affairs of the State, responding to diverse external pressures and at the sametime, having to deal with delivering services immediately for the people to change and impact their lives in a poor and underdeveloped political environment. Why is Sierra Leone, a fantastically rich and natural resource-endowed country, so spectacularly poor?

Governing a Poor Country: Perspectives from a Former Chief Minister of Sierra Leone is a groundbreaking and influential book that examines how and why the Chief Minister of the Republic of Sierra Leone significantly contributed to the effective political and economic management of the state and in the process, raised fundamental questions about the wisdom, constitutionality and efficacy of creating or re-instating an innovative governance structure at the centre of the New Direction administration in Sierra Leone.

Drawing from the governance experience of having served as the Second Chief Minister of the country since its colonial creation, but the First Chief Minister in the Republic of Sierra Leone, Professor David Francis provides a first-hand, brutally candid, critically reflective and indepth insight of the role and mandate of the position of Chief Minister as a governance structure, appointed, assigned and delegated by the President in pursuant of Sections 40, 53 and 56 of the 1991 Constitution of Sierra Leone.

This is not an academic or theoretical book, but a governance policy-practice examination of his stewardship as Chief Minister, in the New Direction administration, outlining what was achieved, the impact of the role as well as the problems and challenges in performing such a high-profile and senior Cabinet role. The book does not set out to blame, accuse or 'name-call' any party, actors and agencies, nor does it disparage or ridicule any political party, but rather reflectively accounts for the relevance and impact of the re-created position of Chief Minister in the governance structure of modern Sierra Leone, 64 years after the governance architecture was first introduced by the British Colonial administration.

The invaluable governance and statecraft lessons derived from this seminal book are applicable to the majority of poor and developing countries grappling with the problems and challenges of how to run a country in Africa and in other parts of the world. The book will be of interest to political leaders running the affairs of the state, academics, scholars, researchers, policy practitioners, diplomats, educators, journalists and others interested in Sierra Leone, African politics and national governance issues.

About the Author

Professor David J. Francis is a distinguished Statesman, internationally recognized academic and policy-practitioner who served as Chief Minister and Minister of Foreign Affairs and International Cooperation of the Republic of Sierra Leone between 2018 – 2023. He is widely accredited for taking Sierra Leone to the United Nations Security Council for the tenure 2024-25, garnering 188 votes globally, the highest on record in Africa. Professor Francis served as the Head of Department of Peace Studies at the University of Bradford in UK and held a Research Professorial Chair in African Peace & Conflict Studies. He is extensively published with 12 books on Sierra Leone and African politics, peace, security and development issues.

"Every political leader or aspiring politician in Africa should read *Governing a Poor Country: Perspectives from a Former Chief Minister of Sierra Leone.* Professor David Francis' thoughtful and provocative practical account of the highs and lows of statecraft in an African country resonates with the problems and challenges of governance in other parts of the Developing *World.*"

Dr Demeke Hassen Mekonnen. Former Deputy Prime Minister and Minister of Foreign Affairs of Ethiopia from 2012 - 2024

"Professor David J. Francis' *Governing a Poor Country: Perspectives from a Former Chief Minister of Sierra Leone* is a timely and insightful contribution to the study of political leadership, governance reform and institutional change in Africa. Drawing from his tenure as Chief Minister, Francis provides a rare insider's perspective on state reform in a fragile, post-conflict environment, blending analytical depth with the practical realities of governance. Francis' book arrives at a pivotal moment in Sierra Leone's national debate on governance".

Professor Dr. John A. D. Alie. Fourah Bay College, University of Sierra Leone

Adonis & Abbey Publishers Ltd
Third Floor
207 Regent Street
London W1B 3HH
Website: http://www.adonis-abbey.com
E-mail Address: editor@adonis-abbey.con

Nigeria:
Unit 1, Vintage Hill Estate Plot No 1368, Guzape District,
Abuja, Nigeria
Tel: +234 7058078841, 234 8052213212

British Library Cataloguing-in-Publication Data
A catalogue record for this book is available from the British Library

ISBN: 9781913976743 (PB)
9781913976750 (HB)

Table of Contents

CHAPTER FIVE

CHAPTER SIX

Map of Sierra Leone

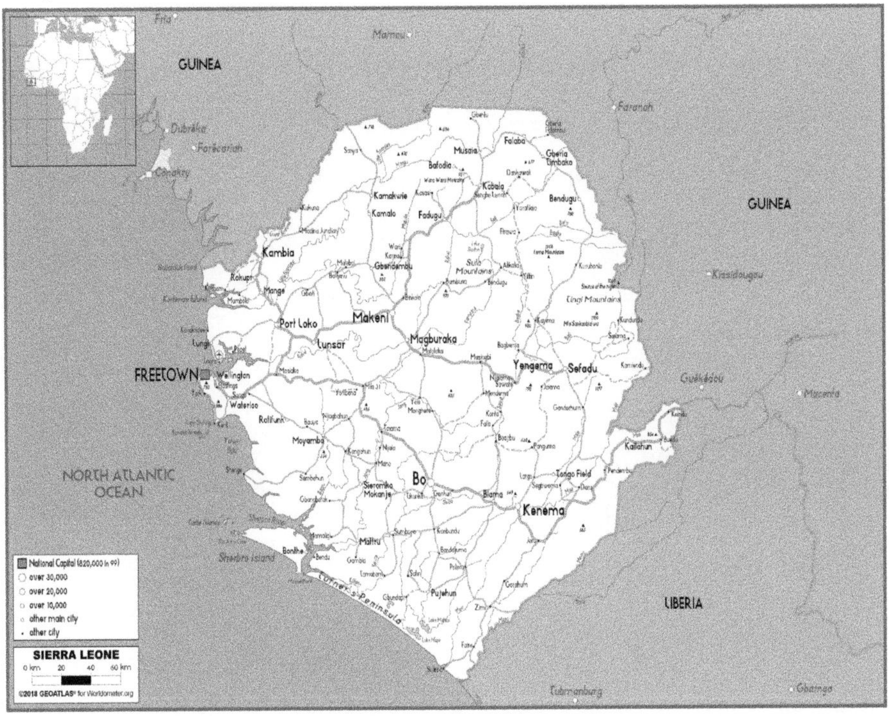

Source: www.https://www.worldometers.info/maps/sierra-leone-road-map-full/

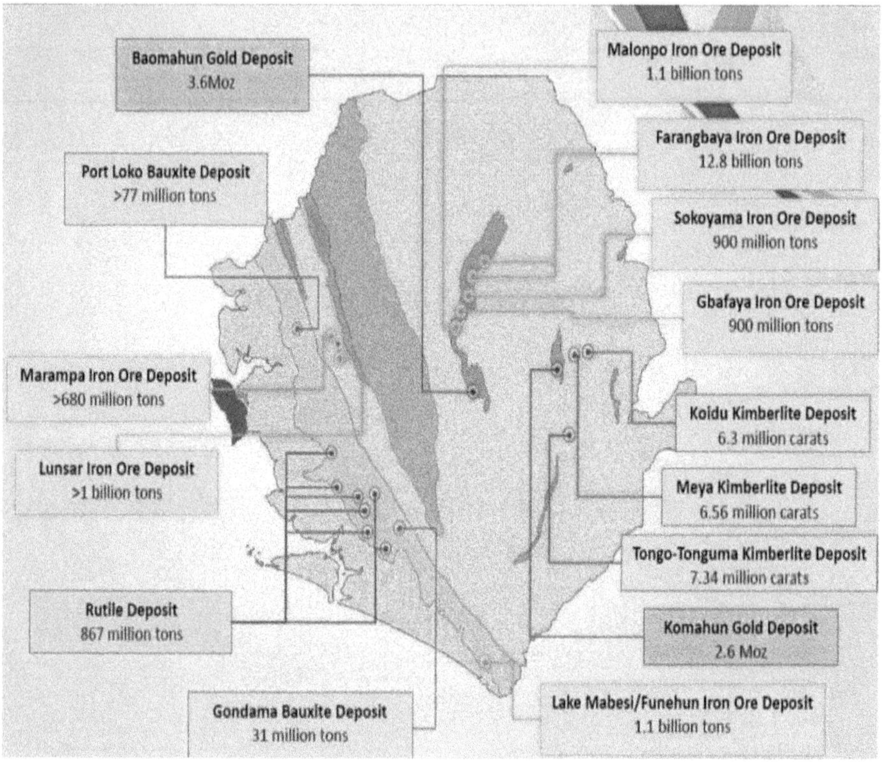

Map of Sierra Leone's National Airborne Geophysical Survey (NAGS) Data on Strategic Minerals Resources 2021, National Mineral Agency, MoMMR

List of Abbreviations

ACC	Anti-Corruption Commission
ACT	Australian Capital Territory
APC	All Peoples Congress
AU	African Union
C-10	African Union Committee of 10 for UNSC Reform
C4C	Coalition for Change
CabSec	Cabinet Secretariat
CCF	City Council of Freetown
CEO	Chief Executive Officer
CISU	Central Intelligence & Security Unit
	Cohesion
COHGM	Commonwealth Heads of Government Meeting
CoI	Commissions of Inquiry
COVID-19	Coronavirus 19
CRF	Consolidated Revenue Fund
	Cultural Organisation
DfID	Department for International Development – UK
DSTI	Directorate for Science, Technology, and Innovation

EC	European Commission
ECOWAS	Economic Community of West African States
EU	European Union
FCO	Foreign & Commonwealth Office – UK
FOCAC	Forum on China–Africa Cooperation
FQE	Free Quality Education
GCFR	Grand Commander of the Federal Republic of Nigeria
GDP	Gross Domestic Product
GoSL	Government of Sierra Leone
GTT	Governance Transition Team
HCD	Human Capital Development
HRMO	Human Resource Management Office
ICPNC	Independent Commission for Peace and National
IMF	International Monetary Fund
MCC	Millennium Challenge Corporation
MDAs	Ministries, Departments, and Agencies
MTNDP	Medium-Term National Development Plan
NAGS	National Airborne Geophysical Survey
NaMED	National Monitoring and Evaluation Directorate

NASSIT	National Social Security and Insurance Trust
NDMA	National Disaster Management Agency
NGC	National Grand Coalition
NGOs	Non-Governmental Organisations
NMA	National Minerals Agency
NPRC	National Provisional Ruling Council
NRA	National Revenue Authority
OBBA	Old Bo School Boys Association
OCM	Office of the Chief Minister
OCM	Office of the Chief Minister
ONS	Office of National Security
OPII	Office of the Presidential Infrastructural Initiative
OSD	Operational Support Division – Sierra Leone Police
PhD	Doctor of Philosophy
PMDU	Prime Minister's Delivery Unit - UK
RMFA	Road Maintenance Fund Agency
RSLAF	Republic of Sierra Leone Armed Forces
SCOP	State Chief of Protocol
SLFA	Sierra Leone Football Association

SLPP	Sierra Leone People's Party
SOEs	State-Owned Enterprises
SRL	Sierra Rutile Limited
STA	Single Treasury Account
TICAD	Tokyo International Conference on African Development
UK	United Kingdom
UN	United Nations
UNDP	United Nations Development Programme
UNESCO	United Nations Educational, Scientific and
UNGA	United Nations General Assembly
UNSC	United Nations Security Council
UNSRSG	United Nations Special Representative of the Secretary General
USA	United States of America
USD	United States Dollar

CHAPTER ONE

Introduction

Governing a Poor Country: Setting the Context

Governing a Poor Country: Perspectives from a Former Chief Minister of Sierra Leone critically assesses the historical evolution, functions, political context, impact, and power politics of the role and mandate of Chief Minister of Sierra Leone as a governance delivery architecture to support the running and political management of the state.

Importantly, this book, written from the perspective of a holder of the Office of Chief Minister in modern Sierra Leone, critically documents and assesses why the role was re-created in post-independent Sierra Leone, 64 years after political independence from the British colonial rule, by the Sierra Leone People's Party (SLPP) New Direction Government[1]. This seminal book examines the role of the Chief Minister and how it functioned as mandated within the purview of Sections 40, 53 and 56 of the Constitution of Sierra Leone; it illustrates the controversies generated by the creation of the role; it also demonstrates and evaluates the differences between the functions of the Chief Minister in the New Direction Government and the roles of the Chief Minister of the British colonial administration; demonstrates how the inter-play of power politics enabled the effectiveness of the role or undermined, if not, made the role redundant in its core mandate to supervise, monitor, coordinate and performance manage Government of Sierra Leone (GoSL) ministries and legislative agencies within the Office of the President.

To fully grasp the significance and impact of the Chief Minister's role, one must first recognise it as a political appointment—specifically, a senior Cabinet position—made by the President. Importantly, it

---

[1] The SLPP is not only the oldest political party in Sierra Leone but also one of the oldest across Africa, established on 27th April 1951, with the motto 'One Country, One People', with 'Green' as the party colour. Its inaugural party chairman was Dr. Milton Margai, a British-trained medical doctor, turned politician advocating for self-rule and political independence from British colonial rule.

operates and functions within a political economy context based on what political scientists describe as a neo-patrimonial or patron-clientelist system of governance. In such polities, politics and governance are fundamentally driven by the pursuit of access to state power and the subsequent control of its resources. These domestic political realities and governance considerations, no matter how experienced, competent, educated, professional, disciplined, and astute the post holder may be, determine the effectiveness, success, and failure of the role of Chief Minister.

Furthermore, the role of the Chief Minister is essentially technocratic, centered on the delivery of governance. As such, the position demands a technocrat and a professional administrator rather than a career politician or a political aspirant. The high-profile nature of the role of Chief Minister, often equated with that of a quasi-Prime Minister, creates a particular problem in that a power-hungry politician with vaulting ambition will be tempted to neglect and even abandon the technocratic and governance delivery functions and mandate and, instead assumes a visible political, if local, politician posture, with a tendency to 'lord' the senior role over colleague ministers appointed by the president.

Setting the Context: Sierra Leone Has No Business Being Poor & the Nature of Domestic Politics

To understand the role and impact of the position of the Chief Minister in the modern governance architecture of Sierra Leone, it is important to set the context and basic knowledge of the country. To this end, the context will briefly outline the political history and development of Sierra Leone, why and how the country has emerged as a poor and least developed nation, and how the post-colonial nature of domestic politics based on neo-patrimonialism and the negative political and socio-development culture have all coalesced to convert Sierra Leone into one of the poorest and least developed nations in the world, ranked 185 out of 193 countries, according to the UNDP Human Development Index Report (2025)[2].

---

[2] UNDP Human Development Report 2025, 'A Matter of Choice: People and Possibilities in the Age of AI,' UN Publications, New York.

Why is Sierra Leone described as a poor and underdeveloped country? Is Sierra Leone a poor country, beyond the basic UN development-oriented definition of poverty? By all indications, Sierra Leone is classified as a poor country and meets all the absolute and relative definitions of poverty and depressing socio-economic and development indicators in terms of lack of financial resources for more than 60 per cent of the population to meet their basic existential necessities such as food, shelter, and healthcare; deprivation; social exclusion; extremely low life expectancy; limited opportunities; and lack of meaningful participation in the decisions that affect their lives.

The important question is, has modern Sierra Leone always been poor and underdeveloped? The simple answer is no! For a start, Sierra Leone is a resource-rich country with vast natural resources and abundant strategic mineral resources, including diamonds, gold, bauxite, rutile, iron ore, limonite, platinum, chromite, coltan, tantalite, lithium, and rare earth minerals, with the legendary 'Star of Sierra Leone', a 968.9-carat diamond, discovered in 1972 and the 'Peace Diamond', a 709-carat diamond discovered in 2017. In fact, the 2021 map of the National Airborne Geophysical Survey (NAGS) data paints a verifiable and evidence-based picture of the abundant strategic minerals of Sierra Leone (see Map 2). The NAGS data shows how Sierra Leone is fantastically rich in natural resources. To illustrate this, the NAGS map shows that in just one small location in the northern part of Sierra Leone at the Farangbaya iron ore deposit, the site has an estimated 12.8 billion tons of verified Iron Ore deposit. A quick mathematical calculation will show that if the current market price (August 2025) of iron ore is USD $105 per ton, then the total value of 12.8 billion tones of iron ore is worth USD $1.344 trillion.

What is more, at independence from the British Colonial administration on 27th April 1961, the socio-political and development of Sierra Leone was seen by international observers and political analysts as more promising than South Korea. Today, South Korea, a relatively small country with a population of 51.7 million, is one of the most developed countries and advanced economies in the world, the 12th largest economy, with a GDP of USD $1.87 trillion, while Sierra Leone, with a population of 7.8 million and a GDP of USD $8.3 billion (2025) as well as a GDP per capita income of USD $873 (2024), is classified as one of the poorest and underdeveloped countries in the world.[3]

With the dawn of political independence, Sierra Leone inherited the enviable history of having served as the seat and centre of the British colonial administration and business in West Africa, running the political and economic affairs of the West African colonial governments from Freetown, Sierra Leone, since 1843.[4] This is not surprising because Sierra Leone became the first Crown Colony of Britain in sub-Saharan Africa in 1808. With this distinction, colonial Sierra Leone became the hub of British colonial administration in West Africa with significant colonial infrastructural development in the country such as the construction of the first railway in West Africa in 1898; the first electricity and broadcasting Services in 1927 in the sub-region; the first country in sub-Saharan Africa to have an airline and airport at Hasting in Freetown in 1927; the first country in British colonial West Africa to have a Tropical Hospital in 1925; first hospital for the mentally retarded in 1920; the first Primary School in 1794 and a University, Fourah Bay College, in 1827; the first country in West Africa where Motor Vehicles were introduced in 1912; the first country in British colonial West Africa to have the English Legal system with black / 'local' judges and jurors as well as serving as the Supreme Court and final Court of Appeal for the Gambia, Nigeria and Ghana; the Freetown Municipality became the first West African colonial city to have a Mayor and the first Banking system, the 'Bank of British West Africa' and the first Post Office in colonial British West Africa.[5]

It becomes obvious that, at independence from British colonialism, Sierra Leone inherited a relatively well-established socio-development

---

[3] UNDP Human Development Index Report 2025, 'A Matter of Choice: People and Possibilities in the Age of AI', UNDP Publication 2025; UNDP 2025, 'Towards 2025 Human Development Report (HDR) / Sierra Leone', UNDP Publication, NY; World Bank, 'Sierra Leone: Country Climate and Development Report', Country June 2025, World Bank Publication, Washington DC; World Bank, 'Sierra Leone Country Economic Memorandum', June 2025, World Bank Publication, Washington DC.

[4] The British West Africa colonial territories administered from Sierra Leone were Nigeria, Gold Coast (Ghana), and Bathurst, Gambia.

[5] Joe A. D. Alie, Sierra Leone Since Independence: History of a Postcolonial State, New Edition, 2015; Christopher Fyfe, A Short History of Sierra Leone, OUP, 1962; C. Magbaily Fyfe, The History of Sierra Leone: A Concise Introduction, Evans Africa, 1981.

infrastructure that could have supported the progressive development of the country as a modern, liberal, progressive, and developed state, similar to that of South Korea.

However, it will be wrong to use the colonial development infrastructure and the Westminster political system bequeathed to post-colonial Sierra Leone as, on the whole, good for the country. We all know that colonialism and colonial governance in Sierra Leone were not for the benefit of the country and Sierra Leoneans but primarily for the benefit of Britain. Colonialism in Sierra Leone and across much of Africa and the rest of the world was a violent, brutal, authoritarian, anti-democratic, exploitative, and extractive process of resource accumulation for Britain and the United Kingdom. Whatever infrastructural developments were made in Sierra Leone were simply to enhance and facilitate the colonial exploitation and extraction of resources from the country. It is therefore not surprising that the majority of the critical infrastructures developed were mainly in Freetown, which provided access to the port—the third-best natural harbour in the world—with easy shipping access and shorter flight times to England and Europe. The provincial regions of Sierra Leone were subjected to systemic neglect by the British colonial administration. At independence, Sierra Leone secured only political freedom and independence. The colonial economic exploitation, development structures, political legacies, and structural conditions remain intact to serve the vested neo-colonial and neo-imperialistic interests of the British colonial masters and the Western-centric political and economic order that emerged with the end of the Second World War and the emergence of the Cold War politics.

Moreover, the colonial constitutional arrangements and laws of the land designed to govern colonial Sierra Leone and the people of the country, such as the Crown Colony constitution of 1808, the 1863 Blackhall constitution, the 1895 constitution, the 1924 constitution, the 1951 Beresford-Stooke constitution, and the 1961 Independence constitution, were all designed to be authoritarian, extractive, and exploitative social contract constitutions to coerce the consent of the subject peoples in the country and further entrench the colonial exploitation of Sierra Leone. I have argued that "Sierra Leone was nothing more than a valuable and lucrative piece of real estate for the British Empire, and the extractive social contract constitutions were designed to achieve this fundamental motivation."[6] This is not surprising because the British colonial government in England formally recognised the original settlement for free slaves in Sierra Leone as a charter to the Sierra Leone Company; in effect, the very first form of government for Sierra Leone was a company rule. Based on this observation, the pointed question is what do companies do best? They exploit for profit!

Why is Sierra Leone, a fantastically rich and natural resource-endowed country, so spectacularly poor? A major factor responsible for the description of contemporary Sierra Leone as a poor and underdeveloped country has to do with the nature of domestic politics based on neo-patrimonial governance. In this context, there is no distinction between the public (res publica, as it pertains to the public realm of the state) and the private realm of the state and governance. In the context of Sierra Leone and across Africa, this type of prebendal politics creates an informal system of governance that informalises and privatises all the state governing institutions to serve the vested interests of those in power, leading to bad governance, rampant corruption, and state capture. All the critical State governing institutions such as the legislature/parliament, the judiciary, the security and defence agencies and key elements of the executive branch of the government including ministers, heads of government parastatals and legislated agencies, are all beholden to and answerable to the president or presidency (president, vice president, office of the president headed by secretary to the president, the first lady, the office of the chief minister).

The primary purpose of politics and governance in this context of neo-patrimonial governance is not about the efficient political and economic management of the state or the delivery of socio-economic development priorities for the people, but essentially about the access to and capture of State power and then using this for patrimonial accumulation and embezzlement of State resources.[7] Those elected by

---

[6] David J. Francis (ed). Peace, Democracy & Development in Africa, Adonis & Abbey, 2016, p.73.

[7] For a detailed understanding of the concept and practice of neo-patrimonial governance and prebendal politics in Sierra Leone, please see: David J. Francis, The Politics of Economic Regionalism: Sierra Leone in ECOWAS, Ashgate, 2001, pp.82-87 & 123 - 130; Uniting Africa: Building Regional Peace & Security Systems, Ashgate/Routledge, 2006, pp. 51 -53

the people, in the context of the dominant political parties in Sierra Leone, the SLPP and the All Peoples Congress (APC)[8], have historically privatised and subverted the state governing institutions for private gains and profit. In this patron – clientelistic context of governance, the ensuing 'Shadow State'[9] becomes nothing more than a 'market' whereby those in control of the 'Official State' are more interested in 'primitive accumulation' of State resources and the politics of decline and underdevelopment of what the former President of Sierra Leone, Siaka Stevens, once described as 'Where a cow is tethered, there it grazes' / '*Usai U Tie Cow Nar de ei for Eat*'.

Within this neo-patrimonial governance context, the Chief Minister functions as a senior Cabinet member and one of the principal advisor to the President. This role is underscored by a fundamental national imperative: Sierra Leone is a resource-rich nation with no justification for its continued state of poverty or underdevelopment. In effect, the contemporary situation of poverty and underdevelopment in modern Sierra Leone is not because of the absence of natural resources, strategic minerals, financial and human resources, but because of the persistent problem of leadership and leadership failure, creating the context of bad governance; prebendal state capture; Western and external control of state power and resources; ethnocratic or tribalistic politics of decline; and the ineffective political and economic management of the state and its resources. It is in this context of the nature of domestic politics that the role and impact of the position of Chief Minister should be evaluated and understood in modern Sierra Leone and the SLPP New Direction Government of President Bio.

---

8 The APC, as the main opposition political party, was established on 20th March 1960, with 'Red' as the party colour and Mr Siaka Stevens, a mines unionist, as its first chairman. The APC ruled Sierra Leone from 1968 to 1992 and 2007 to 2018, with the period from 1978 to 1992 as a one party dictatorship under Siaka Stevens and Joseph Saidu Momoh.

9 William Reno, Corruption and State Politics in Sierra Leone, Cambridge University Press, 1998.

Relational Context and Impact on Governance

An important background and context that needs to be highlighted is my previous relationship with President Bio before his election and assumption of leadership of the country as well as the critical roles that I played after the SLPP won the general and presidential elections on 4th April 2018.

Firstly, in January 2014 I officially became the principal research supervisor for the PhD degree/Doctoral studies of Julius Maada Bio at the University of Bradford in the United Kingdom. I was then the substantive Head of the Department of Peace Studies, the world's largest and most renowned academic and research centre of excellence in peace and conflict studies. I was also the director of the John & Elnora Ferguson Centre for African Studies, based in the Department of Peace Studies, managing the £1.75 million grant to the University of Bradford. As a senior academic and research professor, with a research professorial chair in African peace and conflict studies and the UNESCO chair for peace education in Africa, the first-ever African to hold two prestigious professorial chairs in the UK, I had significant academic and intellectual clout and was esteemed in England because of my academic scholarship and high-level international policy practice work (consultancies and advisory roles) with Western and African governments as well as intergovernmental and multilateral organisations such as UN agencies, the EU, the African Union, the ECOWAS and research/policy-relevant think tanks. Naturally, my academic pedigree, managerial leadership of the department, and high-profile status at the University of Bradford as the institution's leading African academic all positively rubbed off on the doctoral candidate/PhD student, Julius Maada Bio.

To his credit, Julius Maada Bio was highly respected by his peers and the doctoral students research community in the Department and the Faculty of Social Sciences because of his unassuming demeanor and the fact that he actively engaged in the research and academic life of the research students community, doing all that was expected of him as a doctoral candidate. During this period, I made sure that our official relationship was professional, with disciplined commitment to the submission of mandatory essays and draft chapters of his thesis. Obviously, he was often 'distracted' by his political ambition to lead the SLPP as presidential candidate/flag bearer for the 2018 presidential elections. He successfully completed and passed with merit his Research

Methods postgraduate degree and also successfully transferred to complete his doctoral research degree in November 2016. It was at this stage that he requested from the university a formal suspension of his doctoral programme of study to enable him to contest the SLPP flag bearer position, which he successfully achieved in 2017.

Why is this background important? This context of academic supervision in a foreign land (England) and professional setting provided a significant backdrop to my subsequent working relationship with President Bio, serving as his Chief Minister. We developed a close but professional, highly respectful, and friendly working relationship, albeit at the level of a supervisor – research student relationship. During this period, we developed the parametres and the imperative for professionalism, competence and disciplined commitment to work delivery outcomes and expectations, devoid of the usual 'padipadi' (overtly friendly) and informalised nature of governance interactions among government/public officers in Sierra Leone.

On a personal level, we developed a very close, respectful, and trusted friendship to the extent that Julius Maada Bio became a 'member' of my family in Bradford, and he was particularly fond of my son, Daniel Francis, and daughter, Ella Francis, always warmly commending their academic and athletic excellence, to the extent that both Daniel and Ella often referred to him as 'Uncle Julius'. This professional and disciplined relationship, backed by our close and respectful friendship, became an important anchor in my role as Chief Minister and my interaction with President Bio.

President Bio had the unique opportunity and firsthand knowledge of my status as a highly respected and distinguished international academic and scholar as well as my competent senior leadership and management in England, albeit in an academic setting. Needless to say I used this strategic advantage to introduce and establish high-level networks, international travel and speaking engagements in England for the doctoral candidate, Julius Maada Bio, such as the October 2016 London-based Chatham House speaking engagement.

Secondly, after the end of my tenure as Head of Department in July 2016, and confident that Julius Maada Bio and the SLPP will win the 2018 presidential and general elections, based on the perspectives of my international network partners that I have been consulting for and providing advisory services to, I took my long overdue sabbatical to come to Sierra Leone to support the political efforts and election campaigns of the SLPP and the presidential candidate/flag bearer, Julius Maada Bio. To avoid conflict of interest, given the political sensitivities of my high-profile roles, I provided informal and covert support for the campaign of presidential candidate Julius Maada Bio. This strategic and politico-intellectual support was highly appreciated by the Presidential Candidate, Julius Maada Bio, and his senior campaign team. Julius Maada Bio even provided an office space for me at his residence at Juba in Freetown to work from and enabled me to significantly contribute to the draft and completion of the SLPP New Direction Manifesto[10] as well as prepare confidential dossiers for the attention of the international community and diplomatic partners in the country, detailing and documenting, with evidence-based factual pictures the APC election violence perpetuated against SLPP supporters and how the ruling APC government used the state security agencies, the police /OSD, and the military to intimidate the SLPP leadership and supporters across the country.

As the confidence of the SLPP leadership increased about the prospect of winning the presidential and general elections in 2018, Julius Maada Bio gave me increasing visibility, and I assumed the de facto role as Senior Adviser to the Presidential Candidate. I was often asked to join high-level meetings with the international community, i.e., the diplomatic and development partners in the country. On critical and sensitive, if not explosive election-related matters, I was often part of the presidential candidate's delegation, such as the Bintumani Hotel meetings in the run-up to the elections. Though not an appointed or elected member of the SLPP National Executive and Campaign team, as Senior Advisor, I played a critical advisory role at the SLPP Elections Campaign Management 'Command Centre' in Freetown, at the Peninsular Road Office, now the Office of the First Lady. I played a dominant role in preparing the Flag Bearer, Julius Maada Bio, for the February 2018 presidential debate at the Bintumani Conference Centre. I did not only write the speech but also extensively prepared the flag bearer, Julius Maada Bio, to master his presentation and confidently

[10]Mr Jacob JusuSaffa, later Minister of Finance and Chief Minister, led on the drafting and completion of the New Direction SLPP People's Manifesto. His Manifesto Team included Dr. Abass Bundu, later Speaker of Parliament. I significantly framed the 2018 New Direction Manifesto political ideology of the SLPP as 'Social Democracy'

deliver his central campaign message, including the now famous campaign mantra:

> If you want free Education, Vote Julius Maada Bio and the SLPP Party.
> If you want to end corruption and Mismanagement of the State, Vote Julius Maada Bio and the SLPP Party.

As a matter of fact, even before my appointment as Chief Minister, I was already exerting important influence and moderation on the campaign focus and strategy of the presidential candidate, especially encouraging the team to focus on professionalism, discipline, and accountability. Obviously, this was not accommodated by the 'close allies' of the presidential candidate who have been used to doing things the '*SaLone way*', as they often reminded me, sarcastically retorting that, '*Professor, dis nor to England you dae*'/ 'Professor, you are not living in England'.

Notwithstanding, I was confident that I had the solid support of the presidential candidate and I also went out of my way to build trust and confidence in facilitating cordial, amicable, and mutually beneficial working relationships with all members of the campaign team. I was quick to realise that some of the senior and older advisers and friends of the presidential candidate already believed and behaved as if they owned the flag bearer, Julius Maada Bio. My presence therefore served two important and strategic functions for the presidential candidate. First, I provided independent and trusted strategic advice to Julius Maada Bio, devoid of the sentiments and 'interest-driven' pieces of advice often given. Second, my presence was highly appreciated and regarded by both the campaign team and, in particular, the presidential candidate, Julius Maada Bio, because my high profile and respected international image, status, and reputation were used to burnish the national and international image of the flag bearer, Julius Maada Bio, in the run-up to the general and presidential elections.

Indeed, well before my appointment as Chief Minister, I had strategically exerted significant informal influence within the SLPP campaign. This leverage proved instrumental not only in securing the party's victory but also in laying the groundwork for a fundamental shift in the nation's governance. As was expected, even at this stage, the battle lines had already been drawn before my appointment as Chief Minister, and this context was to determine the level of cooperation, support, and/or animosity I experienced from some of those colleagues who were appointed to serve in the New Direction government of President Bio.

Thirdly, on 5th April 2018, I was appointed as the Chairman of the Governance Transition Team to conduct an audit and stocktaking exercise to assess the fiscal and governance health of the country at the time when the SLPP and President Bio assumed the reins of power from the outgoing President Koroma's APC administration. Understandably, my appointment as the Chairman of the Governance Transition Team was greeted with overwhelming national public interest because I was not part of the usual and mainstream political class or a local party politician, but an academic who had not been residing in the country. I was bemused by the national curiosity and local media frenzy generated by my appointment as the GTT Chairman.

Fourthly, during the period between my appointment as the GTT Chairman and my subsequent appointment as Chief Minister in May 2018, I was the de facto speechwriter for the newly elected President Bio. This was not surprising because the close advisers and the newly elected president expected me to write his speeches because with all the euphoria and political enthusiasm of a newly elected president and political party, the majority of the people never bothered about or even had the calm and rational head to simply remember that the newly elected president had to speak to the nation by giving speeches. To this end I wrote the following presidential speeches:

i. Swearing-in Ceremony of H. E. President Julius Maada Bio as the newly elected President of the Republic of Sierra Leone on 5th April 2018 at the Radisson Blu Hotel[11];
ii. the Commemoration of the 57th Independence Anniversary at the Siaka Stevens National Stadium on 27th April 2018;
iii. OBBA Celebrations in Bo on 15thApril 2018.

[11] All presidential swearing ceremonies are held at the State House, the seat of government. In this particular instance, we, i.e., the presidential candidate, Julius Maada Bio, and family, including close advisers, found ourselves in this usual situation of finding 'refuge and safety' from the ruling APC violence and intimidation in the secure and well-guarded comfort of the Radisson Blu Hotel in Freetown, where the newly elected president had been staying. It was agreed that the Chief Justice should swearin the new President at the Raddison Hotel to avoid the 'drama' and security concerns of traveling to and hosting the ceremony event at the State House.

Outline of Book

How to run a country? This is the challenge faced by political and economic leaders entrusted with running the affairs of the state, responding to diverse external pressures, and at the sametime, having to deal with delivering services immediately for the people to change and impact their lives in a poor and underdeveloped political environment. *Governing a Poor Country: Perspectives from a Former Chief Minister of Sierra Leone* is a groundbreaking and influential book that examines how and why the Chief Minister of the Republic of Sierra Leone significantly contributed to the effective political and economic management of the state and, in the process, raised fundamental questions about the wisdom, constitutionality, and efficacy of creating or re-instating such an innovative governance structure at the centre of the New Direction administration in Sierra Leone.

Drawing from the governance experience of having served as the second chief minister of the country since its colonial creation, but the first chief minister in the Republic of Sierra Leone, I provide a first-hand, brutally candid, critically reflective, and in-depth insight into the role and mandate of the position of chief minister as a governance structure, appointed, assigned, and delegated by the president in pursuit of Sections 40, 53, and 56 of the 1991 Constitution of Sierra Leone.

This is not an academic or theoretical book, but a governance policy-practice examination of my stewardship as Chief Minister in the New Direction administration, outlining what was achieved and, the impact of the role as well as the problems and challenges in performing such a high-level and senior cabinet role. The book does not set out to blame, accuse, or 'name-call' any party, actors, or agencies, nor does it disparage or ridicule any political party, but aims rather to reflectively account for the relevance and impact of the re-created Chief Minister role in the governance structure of modern Sierra Leone, 64 years after it was first introduced by the British Colonial administration.

This seminal book is outlined in six chapters. With the setting of the context in Chapter 1, Chapter 2 examines the historical evolution of the role and mandate of the Chief Minister and its re-creation in modern Sierra Leone during the SLPP New Direction administration in 2018 as an innovative governance structure. Chapter 3 outlines and assesses the diverse and numerous roles and responsibilities of the New Direction government chief minister including serving as presidential advisor, coordinating and follow-up, supervisory and monitoring, organising governance delivery retreats and ministerial performance management, and leading on strategic policy and national institution building responsibilities. In Chapter 4, the primary focus is on how and why the Chief Minister led the establishment of building national governance institutions such as the National Disaster Management Agency, Bintumani III National Dialogue for National Cohesion, and the Independent Commission for Peace and National Cohesion, including the politics of the parliamentary ratification of these state institutions. Chapter 5 provides a critical insight into the much less-talked-about but visible roles of the Chief Minister, such as serving as Special Emissary and the international engagement role assigned or delegated by the President. Chapter 6 concludes with indispensable lessons in statecraft and how the prebendal nature of domestic politics and corrosive political culture perpetually undermine the role and mandate of the Chief Minister and, in the process, limit the impact and relevance of technocratic governance in the efficient political and economic management of the state.

The invaluable governance and statecraft lessons derived from this seminal book are applicable to the majority of poor and developing countries grappling with the problems and challenges of how to run a country in Africa and other parts of the world. The book will be of interest to political leaders running the affairs of the state, academics, scholars, researchers, policy practitioners, diplomats, educators, journalists, and others interested in Sierra Leone and African politics and governance issues.

CHAPTER TWO

The Evolution of the Office of the Chief Minister: Historical Context and Functions in Modern Sierra Leone

Introduction

Chapter 2 critically examines the historical evolution and contextual roles of the Chief Minister's office in Sierra Leone. It traces this developmental trajectory from the era of British colonial rule through the transition to a modern Republican state, culminating in an analysis of the role's function within President Julius Maada Bio's New Direction administration. The chapter historically confirms that though Dr. Milton Margai was the first holder of the post of Chief Minister during the colonial era in 1954, Professor David Francis is the second holder of the post and title of Chief Minister in the history of Sierra Leone, but importantly, the first holder of the post and title of Chief Minister since political independence in 1961. The chapter outlines the key roles and mandate of the Chief Minister as a senior presidential appointee vested with duties and responsibilities assigned by or delegated by the president pursuant to Sections 40, 53, and 56 of the 1991 Constitution. Chapter Two importantly advances, based on practical governance experience, some of the key leadership characteristics needed to effectively deliver in the role as Chief Minister, while at the same time operating in the challenging context of the negative nature of domestic politics and political culture based on neo-patrimonial governance. The chapter further examines the additional multiple roles and responsibilities undertaken, such as de facto presidential speech writer and the chairman of the Governance Transition Team (GTT).

Chief Minister: Historical Evolution from Colonial Rule to Modern Sierra Leone

The role of Chief Minister was first introduced in 1954 by the British colonial government as the leader of the majority party in the Legislative Assembly and headed the Executive Council. The colonial chief minister was assigned several ministerial portfolios, including agriculture, health, and forests. As Head of Government in colonial Sierra Leone, the Chief Minister led the members of the Executive Council of Ministers, appointed from the SLPP majority party after the elections. The colonial Chief Minister played an important role in governing the country and preparing the path for self-rule and national independence. A key responsibility of the Chief Minister was to mobilise the diverse political parties, interest groups, and progressive forces in the country and to promote national unity for the attainment of political independence.

The British colonial administration was very clear about the mandate and responsibilities of the role of Chief Minister and included leading the Executive Council and directing, monitoring, and overseeing the various departments/ ministries of government. The 1951 Beresford-Stooke Constitution created the legal and constitutional mandate for the appointment of the Chief Minister to head the Executive Council and granted ministerial oversight over various sectors of government. In actual fact, the mandate of the Chief Minister included two broad principal functions, which were to support the running of the colonial government as head of the Executive Council and to prepare the country for the attainment of national political independence.

The first holder of the office of Chief Minister was Dr. Milton Margai, who was then the leader of the majority party in the colonial Legislative Assembly. The SLPP won the 1951 and 1957 elections to the Legislative Council. The Chief Minister was appointed by the Governor General, i.e., the local representative of the British monarch, and exercised most of the powers governing Sierra Leone. Dr. Milton Margai served in the role as Chief Minister from 1954 to 1958. The constitutional changes in 1956 replaced the Legislative Assembly with the House of Representatives and the Executive Council. Reformed in 1958, it changed the title of Chief Minister to Premier, with Milton Margai appointed to this role, but with the same functions as Chief Minister.

At independence on 27th April 1961, the title of Chief Minister/Premier was transformed to Prime Minister, and Sir Dr. Milton Margai continued in this role until his death in 1964. The title of Office of Prime Minister and Head of Government was abolished in 1978 after the All Peoples Congress (APC) party constitutional referendum that introduced a one-party state.

The SLPP New Direction Government and the Re-creation of the Office of Chief Minister

On 30th April 2018, the State House Press Secretary announced that I have been appointed by President Bio to serve as the Chief Minister of the SLPP New Direction Government, a senior Cabinet Minister. The Secretary to the President, Mr Denis Vandy, in a letter dated 2nd May 2018, stated, 'I have the honour to inform you that, in accordance with Section 56 of the Constitution of Sierra Leone 1991, it has pleased His Excellency the President, Brigadier (Rtd.) Julius Maada Bio, to appoint you as Chief Minister subject to the approval of Parliament'.[1] A subsequent letter from the Secretary to the Cabinet and Head of the Civil Service, Dr. Julius Sandy, dated 14th May 2018, stated, 'Following your appointment by His Excellency the President and your subsequent subscription to the Oath of Office of Minister, I now forward, hereto attached, Conditions of Service appertaining to the said appointment'.[2] President Bio, in confirming my appointment as a senior member of Cabinet, stated in a letter dated 9th May 2018, 'To Professor David J. Francis, whereas it is provided by subsection (1) of section 56 of the Constitution that there shall be, in addition to the Office of the Vice-President, such other offices of Ministers and Deputy Ministers as may be established by the President. Now, therefore, in the exercise of the powers vested in me by subsection (1) of section 56 of the Constitution and all other powers thereunto enabling me, I do hereby appoint you as Chief Minister to be a Member of the Cabinet from the date, subject to the provision of the said Constitution'.[3]

On my appointment and having successfully gone through Parliamentary Approval, I was required to subscribe to the Oath of Minister of the Government of Sierra Leone. In subscribing to the Oath as Minister in the presence of the President at State House, I committed to: 'I Professor David J. Francis, do hereby in the name of God/Allah

---

1 Office of the Secretary to the President, Letter to Professor David J. Francis, Chief Minister-Designate, GoSL, 30th April 2018

2 Appointment of Chief Minister Letter, Office of the President, Freetown, Ref: SF/OP/50/294/01. Conditions of Service for Ministers, Cabinet Secretariat, Ref: CSF/209

3 Office of the President, State House, Letter of Appointment from Secretary to the President, 9 May 2018.

(swear) (solemnly affirm) that I will faithfully and truly discharge the duties of the Office of the Chief Minister of the Republic of Sierra Leone, and that I will support, uphold, and maintain the Constitution of Sierra Leone as by law established, So help me God/Allah.'[4]

The President also specifically assigned my role as Chief Minister in a letter dated 9th May 2018, stating that 'In the exercise of the powers vested in me by subsection (5) of section 56 of the Constitution of Sierra Leone 1991, I have the pleasure of assigning to you the portfolio of Chief Minister'.[5] As such, the SLPP New Direction government of President Bio reinstated the position of Chief Minister, 64 years after it was first created by the British colonial administration.

As Chief Minister and as a senior Cabinet Minister, I became a member of the Defence Council and the National Security Council. In subscribing to the Defence Council's Oath of Official Secrecy, I stated thus: 'I, Professor David J. Francis, Chief Minister, Office of the President, hereby affirm that I should not divulge any classified or official information gained by me as a result of the position I hold in the Public Service to any unauthorised person, either orally or in writing, without the prior official approval of the Chairman of the Defence Council, to whom written application should be made for such approval'.[6]

As was expected, my appointment as Chief Minister created another controversy and media distractions, with those 'opponents' from both within the SLPP and the main opposition APC party claiming that it was an unconstitutional appointment and that the President had no constitutional powers to create and appoint a Chief Minister.

In fact, the national controversy generated by the re-creation of the role of Chief Minister and my appointment to the post by President Bio was played out in the House of Parliament. During my parliamentary vetting and approval process in the Wells on Parliament on 8th May 2018, Members of Parliament from across the political divide forcefully voiced their support for the wisdom of President Bio for reinstating the position of Chief Minister in modern Sierra Leone as well as reflected the public concerns about the role of Chief Minister.

---

[44] Oath of Office as Minister, Sworn at State House, Freetown on 9th May 2018.
[5]GoSL, State House, Freetown, Sierra Leone, Letter dated 9th May 2018.
[6] Office of the President, Letter from Secretary to the President, 9 May 2018.

Hon. Sahr Charles kicked off the spectacular debate in Parliament by reminding colleagues MPs in the following terms: 'Mr Speaker, Honorable Members, I want to conclude with the proposed Chief Minister, Professor David J. Francis. I want to remind him that his position has become an issue of public debate. This is because a lot of people are of the view that this particular position is not necessary. However, I want to believe that it is in the wisdom of the president to achieve his New Direction agenda he has decided to create that office. You have a task to prove your detractors wrong. It is going to give you a hell of a time, especially when you will be trying to synchronise your duties as chief minister and the duties of the vice president. This is where the big problem lies. But I want to believe that from the responses you provided to the Committee on Appointments and Public Service, you will live up to that expectation'.[7]

It was in this context of controversy and huge expectations that the Leader of Government Business, Hon. Sidi Tunis, proposed my parliamentary approval, stating:

'Mr Speaker, Honourable Members, Professor David J. Francis is a Commissioner/Board of Director of the UK Government Commonwealth Scholarships Commission. He is also the Head of the Department of Peace Studies at the University of Bradford and Director of the University of Bradford's John and Elnora Ferguson Centre for African Studies in UK. He provides high-level strategic leadership, operational management and oversight of the administration and large-scale research and capacity building grant of estimated £2.3 million, including the £1.75 million Ferguson Trust 5-year grant to the Africa Centre / JEFCAS.

Commenting on the difference between the role of the Vice President and Chief Minister, Professor Francis said: "There is no contradiction between the role of the Chief Minister and the role of the Chief Executive and the Vice President. Sections 52, 53 and 54 of the 1991 Constitution of Sierra Leone are very clear. The President is the Head of Government Business and Chief Executive, the Vice President is the Principal Assistant to the President. The role of the Chief Minister is simply to follow-up and coordinate the decisions made by the Chief

[7] Parliamentary Debates (Hansard), Official Hansard Report First Session – First Meeting of the Fifth Parliament of the Second Republic of Sierra Leone, Proceedings of the Sitting of the House Held Tuesday, 8th May 2018, p.

Executive and his Assistant, and to make sure that they are delivered to line Ministries and sectors. This has been the problem in terms of governance because everything leads up to the Presidency. That is a recipe for chaos. The President, in his wisdom, therefore created the Office of the Chief Minister, who is essentially the office messenger of the President and the Vice President. The plan for the role of the Chief Minister is to facilitate and provide competent leadership that will ensure that what has been decided by the President and Vice President are cascaded on to the line ministries for implementation.

Mr Speaker, Honourable Members, for some time now, we have had government Ministers who took positions, but after a month or two, they began mixing politics and governance. Sometimes, they are not even too sure whether they are governing or they are running a political party. I am sure that this is the reason why His Excellency the President, Rtd. Brigadier Julius Maada Bio, has deemed it fit to establish the office of the Chief Minister and has nominated somebody who is equally qualified to man the office. I want to inform the House that the proposed Chief Minister is not a politician. He always tells people thus: "I am not a politician". And he is indeed not a politician but a technocrat'.[8]

Hon. Dr. Kandeh Yumekella, leader of the National Grand Coalition (NGC) party in Parliament, stated, 'We are happy to see the Chief Minister, who is going to occupy a new position in this country. I want to remind him that he is now in a glass, which means that everybody can see him. Based on his job description, he has a tough job to ensure delivery. The people of this country need Sierra Leoneans who can deliver, and this Parliament is ready to serve the government, as we have demonstrated during the interview of the nominees. We are ready to render our help in a constructive manner so that you deliver good policies for this republic'.[9] Similarly, Hon. Bernadette Songa of the SLPP in endorsing her support for my appointment, stated in glowing terms, 'Mr. Speaker, I want to briefly talk about Professor David Francis. I recently had the opportunity to meet him. During my acquaintance with

---

[8] Parliamentary Debates (Hansard), Official Hansard Report First Session – First Meeting of the Fifth Parliament of the Second Republic of Sierra Leone, Proceedings of the Sitting of the House Held Tuesday, 8th May 2018, p.

[9] Parliamentary Debates (Hansard), Official Hansard Report First Session – First Meeting of the Fifth Parliament of the Second Republic of Sierra Leone, Proceedings of the Sitting of the House Held Tuesday, 8th May 2018, p.

him, I realised that he is very disciplined and principled. I personally admire him, and I am sure he is going to be good as Chief Minister. I keep wondering in my mind where this fine gentleman was hiding. I was personally pleased when I saw his name for such a position. I have no doubt that you will deliver, and what we need in this country is not the academia of ministers but the principle and the core values that you stand for'.[10] Perhaps the most forceful but controversial endorsement came from the SLPP Hon Ibrahim Tawa Conteh, categorically affirming that;

> Mr Speaker, Honoruable Members, I start with Professor David J. Francis, proposed Chief Minister. This has been a controversial position and several nomenclatures have been attached to that position. Some have called you the new Prime Minister; others referred to you as the man that has come to usurp the functions of the Office of the Vice President; and some say that you are the President that was not elected. But I want to believe from what I have heard yesterday when you were interviewed that you specifically understand exactly what is required of you. You said you were aware of the fact that Sierra Leoneans are in a hurry to move this country forward. I am confident to report to this House that we have a man who is ready to hit the ground running. We are not here to lavish praises on you because the expectations of the people come through us. However, we must give you hope and we must make you believe that we are supportive of this position and functions attached therein. You are the first person to occupy the Office of the Chief Minister, and I want to state here that the start of any office is not an easy task. However, with your range of experiences, we want to believe that you will be able to serve as the conduit that you said you would serve, so that traders at Abacha Street will not have cause to go to the President when they have issues, but they will come to you as the Chief Minister.[11]

[10] Ibid

[11]Rt Hon. Ibrahim TawaConteh, is Deputy Speaker of Parliament, Ibid. p.71.

Bringing a lucid grasp of national history, extensive political governance experience and constitutionalism, the Speaker of Parliament, Dr Abass Bundu, eruditely settled the debate on my Parliamentary approval stating: 'Honourable Members, today is an Historic day. It marks a milestone in the history of Sierra Leone politics. For the first time since independence in 1961, Parliament is being asked to approve the nomination of a Chief Minister, 'primus inter pares'. . . . This is the first time in the entire history of this country that this House is being asked to approve the Chief Minister. This is what makes it historic; and that is what makes this particular session unique.

Honorable Members, I want to once again take this opportunity to congratulate Professor David Francis for his appointment as Chief Minister. . . .Let us be candid that the task ahead is enormous and is mind bothering. It is awesome and we need all hands on deck to extricate this country from the doldrums. . . . I want to remind Professor David Francis that the Office of the Chief Minister is designed to ensure effectiveness and efficiency in the delivery of services to the people of this country. With your wealth of experience against the background of academia, we have no doubt that you will live up to the expectations of the President and you will live up to the trust this House is prepared to repose in you. . .

Honorable Members, Professor David Francis is going to occupy the third position on the pyramid, next only to the Vice President and the President, as far as the Executive Arm of the Administration is concerned. This is a very great responsibility that he will be carrying. We know you have excelled before in your previous locations, and we know you can do it again this time. You would do it again for the people of this country of which you are truly a part'.[12]

Much later in 2020, the renowned legal luminary, former APC senior minister and former vice president, Dr Abdulia O. Conteh, wrote in Sierra Eye Magazine in March 2020, questioning the appointment of a chief minister by President Bio, dismissing the appointment and the office of chief minister as an 'unconstitutional appointment', as an 'anachronism and a misnomer' but at the same time, equating the 'chief minister' to that of a prime minister, using unverified internet/website sources such as 'Siri' and Wikipedia as the 'sound basis' for his rather

[12] Ibid, pp. 77 – 78.

false equivalence, stating that 'The Prime Minister of Sierra Leone is David Francis since May 8, 2018'.[13]

Nevertheless, I do agree with the reasoned explanation and position of Dr Abdulia Conteh, when he argued that '...the tendency to equate the Office of the Chief Minister to the one that existed in 1961 and to that of the Prime Minister creates the erroneous idea that David Francis is the one who dominates the cabinet and not the president, that David Francis exercises control over the Cabinet's structure, agenda, and meetings and not the President. The tendency to equate the office of the Prime Minister to that of the Chief Minister and the idea that the Chief Minister is serving in the same capacity as the Chief Minister of 1961, whether they are improperly motivated or ill-advised, creates confusion and possibly constitutional questions that can have significant impact upon the exercise of Executive Authority'. [14]

Suffice to say that though the 1991 Constitution does not specifically mention or provide for the role and function of a chief minister, the president in appointing and standing-up the position of Chief Minister, fully utilised the provisions of Section 40 (1), i.e., 'supreme executive authority', and Section 53 (1) on the 'exercise of executive authority', in that 'the executive power in Sierra Leone shall vest in the President and may be exercised by him directly or through members of the cabinet, ministers, deputy ministers, or public officers subordinate to him'.[15]

There was an exaggerated media hype and controversy deliberately orchestrated by those 'close allies' of the then presidential candidate, now President Bio, who were, to put it most charitably, upset with my appointment as chief minister and never appreciated their own respective senior appointments by President Bio. Within Sierra Leone's framework of patron-client politics, the President's 'close allies' expected to be appointed Chief Minister as a matter of course. This sense of entitlement highlighted the friction between traditional political expectations and the President's shift toward a delivery-focused administration. Some of them even claimed that my appointment was ultra vires the constitution and as such beyond the powers of the president to make such a senior and high-profile appointment. In fact,

[13] Basita Michael, 'Pres. Bio Leading But Not in Charge?' SierraEye, March – May 2020, pp. 8 – 12.

[14] Ibid, p. 10.

[15] GoSL, The Constitution of Sierra Leone 1991, p, 49.

these 'internal (SLPP) 'detractors' (and I mean it positively) did everything to prevent my parliamentary approval, erroneously claiming that the role and function of the Chief Minister was a usurpation of the office and mandate of the Vice President.

This was a wrong position politically orchestrated to undermine my assumption of the Office of Chief Minister. Sections 40, 53, and 56 of the 1991 Constitution grant the President the power to make such an appointment. Sections 53 and 54 of the Constitution clearly demarcate the executive authority and powers of the President and that of the Vice President. What is more, these 'internal detractors' made sure that I had to renounce and nullify my British Citizenship[16], before my appointment as Chief Minister was approved by Parliament. The renunciation and nullification of my British citizenship was not a problem for me because it was a constitutional requirement to be fulfilled under Section 76 (a), which explicitly disqualifies dual citizenship from holding parliamentary and ministerial appointments. Section 76(a) states, 'if he is a naturalised citizen of Sierra Leone or is a citizen of a country other than Sierra Leone, having become such a citizen voluntarily, or is under a declaration of allegiance to such a country'.[17] During my parliamentary approval on 8th May 2018, the Rt. Honourable Speaker of Parliament, Dr. Abass Bundu went out of his way to stress in the Wells of Parliament that: 'Honourable Members. . . let it be on the records that, in keeping with the provisions of our national Constitution, Professor David J. Francis is a Sierra Leonean by nationality'.[18] This important clarification was reinforced by the Leader of Government Business, Hon Sidi Tunis, confirming that 'And I want to add that he does not hold a dual nationality'.[19]

Given the high stakes of the New Direction agenda, why did President Bio choose me to spearhead the office of the chief minister? First, President Bio has seen, on first hand basis, my proven leadership ability and my demonstrable track record of firm and assertive

---

[16] Having resided in England for more than 25 years, I acquired British Citizenship and Dual Nationality as a Sierra Leonean and British national.

[17] Sierra Leone Government, The Constitution of Sierra Leone 1991, Government Printing Department, Pg. 65

[18] Parliamentary Debates (Hansard) Official Hansard Report First Meeting of the First Session of the Fifth Parliament of the Second Republic of Sierra Leone, Proceedings of the Sitting of the House Held Tuesday, 8th May 2018, p. 51

[19] Ibid, 8th May 2018, p. 51

leadership, competence, professionalism, and discipline. President Bio needed a highly competent leader to support governance delivery at the centre of the New Direction administration. Having served as Chairman of the Governance Transition Team, President Bio also wanted to showcase a team of highly competent, professional, and accomplished leaders in his new government and cabinet to inspire national confidence and international credibility, instant name recognition and approval. Second, President Bio had earlier appointed me as Foreign Minister-Designate for the purpose of Sierra Leone's participation in the Commonwealth Heads of State and Government Summit in London in April 2018, a function I competently delivered in terms of representing Sierra Leone as Foreign Minister. Third, I realised that President Bio had his own 'political agenda' in that he deliberately appointed me to the role as Chief Minister based in the Office of the President and as one of his principal advisers because he wanted to break free from the shackles of the 'close allies' who had become his handlers and gatekeepers, with an entitlement mentality of 'owning' the President. My appointment as Chief Minister, someone perceived to be an 'outsider' to the neo-patrimonial and 'Shadow State', if not the 'padipadi' (informal and friendly) corrupt governance system of domestic politics, was regarded as a breath of fresh air for President Bio and across the nation, irrespective of the political divide. President Bio was confident that, given my strong leadership and assertive personality with a penchant for professionalism, discipline, and competent delivery, he will be insulated and protected from the vagaries and distractions of the nature of domestic politics that prioritised access to state power and its patrimonial resources.

International observers, in particular, the Western diplomatic and development partners in the country equated the chief minister and the Office of the chief minister as a delivery unit. In fact, my interactions with the UK FCO, DFID,[20] and the Tony Blair Institute and African Governance Initiative (AGI) all tried as much as possible to gently steer me in the direction and substantive operational practice of the concept and practice of a delivery unit in governance service delivery. I resisted this 'direction of travel' because the chief minister and the Office of the

[20] UK Government Ministries including the Foreign and Commonwealth Office (FCO) / Foreign Ministry, and the Department for International Development (DfID)

Chief Minister were significantly different and not a simple delivery unit. To start with, the Office of the Chief Minister is different from the Prime Minister's Delivery Unit (PMDU) established during the tenure of the Premiership of Tony Blair. In fact, Prime Minister Tony Blair only set up the PMDU as the centre of his governance delivery during the start of his second term in office, after he had clarified the strategic delivery priorities of his New Labour government.

In contrast, President Bio's New Direction Government appointed and established the Office of the Chief Minister from the start of the administration as the centre of governance delivery to coordinate, monitor, supervise, follow up, and performance manage the implementation of the government agenda for results and how to assess the impact of delivery outcomes.

To be clear, the concept of Delivery Unit, as originally conceived, attempts to establish a unit or units with the primary focus and mandate to deliver or lead on delivery implementation, rather than focus on policy, planning, and strategy. In other words, the Delivery Unit is about getting things done, or solving the problems and challenges of getting things done and it is influenced by a delivery routine, delivery practice, and delivery mentality. In the context of Sierra Leone, the Office of the Chief Minister is not only about getting things done as a delivery centre, but also ambitiously takes on important governance issues relating to policy, planning, strategy, and implementation.

I have to acknowledge that in setting up the roles and mandate of the Office of the Chief Minister, I was influenced by the concept and practice of the Science of Deliverology as advanced by Sir Michael Barber in his book, *How to Run a Government* (2015). I was further influenced by the practical governance delivery success stories in Ethiopia, Rwanda, and the UK. In establishing the Office of the Chief Minister, I had at the back of my mind the apt reflection of Michael Barber stating,

> ...how to run a government so that it delivers the change it has promised. . . .understanding how to run a government effectively is important because the success or otherwise of governments is fundamental to the prosperity and well-being of all of us, wherever we live. . . . the process of delivery is important to politics since democracy is threatened if politicians repeatedly make promises they don't then deliver; it is also important to the citizens regardless of politics, because

> if governments fails, their lives- education, health, safety, travel and parks, for example, not to mention the effective regulation of markets- are materially threatened.[21]

Upon assuming the office of Chief Minister, I was firmly convinced that the position must be defined as a technocratic mandate rather than a conventional political post. I recognised that the role's success depended on its distance from the maneuvers of mainstream, traditional politics[22]. My understanding was that a technocrat is someone with particular skills, competences, and expertise and is able to 'rationally' use this expertise to deliver tangible results and concerted outcomes for the people to impact and change their lives for the better. While in the role, I often described myself as 'not a politician' but a 'results delivery man' and the 'enforcer', which was not often received well by colleague ministers and the SLPP rank and file.

Notwithstanding, I was aware that 'technocratic governance delivery' does not operate in a political vacuum. Given the challenging context of the nature of domestic politics in Sierra Leone, I desperately needed to demonstrate astute political acumen and judgement as well as an abundant dose of political courage and confidence to take calculated, if not bold and assertive, risks needed to deliver results and assess outcomes and impact.

My appointment as chief minister generated a lot of international interest and commendation of the new government of President Bio. The Foreign Secretary, later Prime Minister of the United Kingdom, the

---

[21] Michael Barber, 'How to Run a Government: So That Citizens Benefit & Taxpayers Don't Go Crazy', Penguin Books, 2015, pp. xi-xiii. M. Barber served as Head of Prime Minister Tony Blair's Delivery Unit in the UK between 2001 – 2005 and Co-founder of Delivery Associates.

[22] As Chief Minister, I was intellectually and ideologically (i.e., Social Democratic values) convinced that there is a moral purpose behind the delivery of targets and results / outcomes and that purpose is to achieve the common good for all, i.e., the desire and effort to change the lives of the people for the better such as providing access to affordable electricity and clean drinking water for all or making sure that children go to School and acquire quality education for free or affordable for the poorest of the poor. Holding the Office of the Chief Minister was not just another job, but a passionate mission to contribute to the common good that benefited all Sierra Leoneans irrespective of the regions, ethnicity, religion and political party.

Rt. Hon. Boris Johnson MP, in his congratulatory letter dated 26th May 2018, stated:

> On behalf of her Majesty's Government, I would like to offer my warmest congratulations to you on your appointment as Chief Minister. I commend Sierra Leone in delivering free, fair and peaceful election…..The United Kingdom remains ready to support the Government of Sierra Leone's vision for development, in response to clear leadership on the delivery of priority reforms. I am delighted that His Excellency President Maada Bio was able to lead a delegation to the Commonwealth Heads of Government Meeting, and it was a pleasure to welcome you to the Commonwealth Foreign Minister's meeting. [23]

Having served in the role as Chief Minister for three years, despite the controversies, there is national consensus across the country and across the party political divide and even among ordinary people that I brought decorum, respectability, professionalism, discipline, strong and assertive leadership, and competence to governance. A senior APC former vice president once said, 'Professor Francis, you brought dignity, respect, and professionalism to the Office of Chief Minister. We may not like you, but the Office of the Chief Minister in modern Sierra Leone will always be associated with your name'.[24]

Risking the perception of arrogance, I maintain the firm conviction that the office of Chief Minister is not a role that just anyone can successfully perform. To endure the unique pressures of the position while delivering tangible governance results, an individual must possess a specific constellation of attributes:

1. Must have the complete trust and confidence of the President and must believe in the President's agenda.
2. Must be the 'Enforcer': A strong, confident, and assertive leader with the temperament to 'Kick-A…..' and the diplomatic skills to cajole colleagues.
3. Ability to politely and diplomatically tell the President what he does not or may not want to hear and to be the bearer of bad news to the President on a consistent, dispassionate, and confidential basis.

---

[23] Foreign & Commonwealth Office, London, Secretary of State, 26th May 2018.
[24] Confidential discussion at State Lodge, Freetown, in August 2024

4. Competent, hardworking, disciplined, focused, and has professional work ethics.
5. Capable of diplomatically and effectively representing the President and Government
6. Demonstrable successful leadership track record, with credibility and integrity
7. Excellent at building relationships, network partnerships, and cross-political party alliances.
8. Politically astute, not to 'outshine the Principal'/ the President and willing to avoid the media limelight as well as able to give credit to others
9. A confident and optimistic attitude to governance and the positive belief that it can be done!
10. Positively command the respect of peers, colleague ministers, and other members of the branches of government, such as the Parliament and Judiciary.
11. A problem-solving mentality/attitude, with the ability to see a silver lining or solution in every governance problem or obstacle.
12. Technocratic, intellectually sound, and analytically grounded to grasp and simplify complex and technical policies and projects
13. Must not be a micromanager but an effective facilitator and delegator of responsibilities and have the ability to attract outstanding and high-performing staff to work in a lean and efficient governance centre.

Against this backdrop, it must be emphasised that a primary objective for appointing a chief minister was to bolster the operational efficiency of the 'Front Office of the Presidency'. By streamlining executive functions, the role serves to safeguard and optimise the President's most finite resource: time. Drawing from the experience of Tony Blair as Prime Minister, he has this to say: 'Time is the most precious commodity. . . .without time to focus on delivery, to work out the right policies, to manage the politics of the change that you're making, you will find that the grand vision you elaborated on so confidently when in opposition will never translate into reality'.[25]

[25] Tony Blair, 'On Leadership: Lessons for the 21st Century', Hutchinson & Heinemann, 2024, p.10

The appointment of a chief minister and the subsequent establishment of the Office of the Chief Minister were motivated by the imperative to create a strong, competent, disciplined, and professional centre at the heart of State House governance operations. It was an attempt to make a clear statement that the New Direction government of President Bio was not 'business as usual', but a departure from the status quo inherited from the APC administration. President Bio and the New Direction government leadership were convinced about the importance of having a strong centre to facilitate and push through service delivery and governance policies. In fact, Tony Blair shared his views on this matter, stating that 'So, the centre of government must be strong enough to help devise policy, ensure strategic coherence, keep the plan on course, communicate it, and above all, deliver on it. There will be crises, things that were never anticipated, events of a supervening nature, scandals, shocks and alarums, and excursions, but throughout, the leader must have a machine relentlessly focused on achieving the objectives set. Make the centre strong!'[26]

As Chief Minister, the Office of the Chief Minister became the de facto 'machine' relentlessly bulldozing the way to get things done and remained 'religiously' focused on achieving the government's agenda and making President Bio succeed. Obviously, in the determined process of doing my work as Chief Minister --- a new way that most of the politicians and civil servants were not used to --- I undoubtedly 'picked up' a number of 'enemies' and 'friend-enemies', who used every opportunity to distract from and undermine the service delivery work and programmes for the people.

However, the desire and principle to establish a 'strong centre' at the heart of the Presidency did not work out in practice; if not, it was a failure. With the approval of the President, the Office of the Chief Minister commissioned the Tony Blair Institute - AGI, with the support of the British High Commission in Freetown, to develop a credible framework and modus operandi, including Standard Operating Procedures (SOP), on how to make the centre of government at State House, i.e., the President and the Presidency, effective and able to efficiently manage the 'Time' of the President. The commissioned report recommended the creation of a new 'Presidential Executive Office' to lead on the following: presidential daily and monthly schedule; daily

[26] Tony Blair, 2024, pp. 14-15.

activities and events; speeches; and external travels. To all intents and purposes, this was a very good governance initiative, but as it is often said, 'good intentions do not always produce the desired outcomes'.

This sound and professional report submitted with important recommendations was quietly set aside and never implemented. To my surprise, I found out that the Office of the Secretary to the President and the Office of SCOP[27], did not take kindly to the recommendations submitted and perceived this as an attempt to usurp the functions of the Secretary to the President relating to managing the 'precious time' and the schedule of the President. However, this perception is fundamentally inaccurate. The functions of the Secretary to the President are explicitly mandated by Section 67 of the Constitution, which establishes the office as the principal administrative head of the presidency and principal adviser to the President. At an implementation meeting convened by the Vice President, Dr Mohamed Juldeh Jalloh, it became obvious to me that the commissioned report was not going to be actioned.

As a matter of fact, the report, despite the funds and time spent to produce it, was never implemented and was quietly shelved. The failure to implement the commissioned report recommendations had an immediate negative impact and created an embarrassing situation for a New Direction administration that constantly touted a change of the poor governance status quo. It happened that on 14th December 2018, the president was booked at 10:00am to attend two separate events on the same day and at the same time. The president was scheduled to deliver a keynote address at the AU-UN Reform C-10 Foreign Minister's meeting at the Radisson Blu Hotel and, at the same time, to participate in the First Lady's 'Hands Off Our Girls' programme at the Bintumani Hotel. At the human and personal level, I understood President Bio's legitimate frustration and the embarrassment to all of us, but at the same time, I took it as a biting indictment on our collective failure to professionalise the management of the president's time and 'front office'. That failure also meant that the president, in some situations, was inappropriately dressed in a safari suit for official state events, simply because he had not seen his daily schedule a day in advance to enable him to be appropriately attired.

To put all of the above analysis into a broader governance perspective, the Office of the Chief Minister is not unique to Sierra

[27] State Chief of Protocol (SCOP)

Leone. For example, the political heads of each of the 31 states of the Republic of India are led by a chief minister, appointed by the state governor, who acts as the leader of the House of the Legislative Assemblies, as provided by the constitution of India. In Pakistan, the Chief Minister is the executive authority and head of the provincial/regional government, as provided by the 1973 constitution of Pakistan, Section 131. In Australia, the head of the Federal government of the Australian Capital Territory (ACT) is the Chief Minister, directly elected by the unicameral Australian Capital Territory Legislative Assembly, as provided for by the Australian Capital Territory / Self-Government Act 1988, section 40. In the context of Australia, the ACT Chief Minister is the equivalent of state premiers and a member of the National Cabinet. To some extent, one would reasonably describe the title of Chief Minister as a relic of British colonial rule and empire across the globe.

New Direction Government Chief Minister: Role and Mandate in Political Governance

Transition from Governance Transition Team Chairman to Assumption of Office of Chief Minister

To fully appreciate the rather peculiar 'road' to the assumption of the appointment as the first Chief Minister in the Republic of Sierra Leone under the New Direction Government of President Bio, we have to understand what I did in 'preparation' for this role since the SLPP won the presidential elections in April 2018 and in the months leading to my substantive appointment as Chief Minister in May 2018. During that short period, I found myself doing several important and high-level governance delivery responsibilities, including serving as principal adviser to the president; supporting the president to put together and finalise a new governance team and cabinet appointments that will inspire confidence in the new administration; assuming the de facto responsibility as speechwriter; chairman of the Governance Transition Team; and serving as foreign minister-designate for the purposes of the Commonwealth Heads of Government Summit in London and the state visit to Qatar in April 2018. Let me elaborate on each of these roles and how they invariably impacted the role of chief minister.

De Facto Presidential Speech Writer: Framing and Influencing the New Direction Government Agenda

With the victory of President Bio on 4th April 2018[28], I found myself, by default, as the de facto presidential speech writer. The president, the close advisers, and the party leaders around the president-elect just assumed and expected that I would write all the official speeches. To deliver this 'unplanned' responsibility, I developed the strategy to always extensively discuss with President Bio to fully understand what he intends to convey and the agenda he wants to set in each of the official speeches that I write. Therefore, I found myself writing the following important speeches: the Oath of Office and Swearing-In on 4th April 2018; London-CHOGM Summit Side-Event on 18th April 2018; 57th Independence Anniversary Address on 27th April 2018; the Presidential Inauguration Address on 12th May 2018; and the OBBA Address on 15th April 2018.

To illustrate the scale and relevance of the agenda-setting motivations of the above speeches, the president captured the prevailing national mood for change and a new direction in the politics and governance of the country. On Wednesday night[29], 4th April 2018, was the swearing-in at the Radisson Blu Hotel, and the president-elect reflected the national euphoria for change, stating, 'This is the dawn of a new era. The people of this great nation have voted to take a new direction'. The new president committed to 'serve as president for all Sierra Leoneans'.[30] The same euphoric message and agenda setting was captured in the president's 57th Independence Anniversary address to the nation on 27th April 2018 at the Siaka Stevens National Stadium, stating that:

---

[28] The SLPP and Presidential Candidate, Julius Maada Bio, won the Presidential run-off with 51.81% and the incumbent APC's Dr Samura Kamara garnering 48.19%.

[29] The 1991 Constitution, Section 42 (3), states that the winner of a Presidential election to be sworn in 'on the same day'.

[30] This was a historic and euphoric moment and I recall after the swearing-in ceremony in the Hotel room of the President, only three of us, i.e., the President, the First Lady-In Waiting, Madam Fatima Bio and I, used the private, if not, privileged moment, to spiritually reflect, giving thanks to God Almighty for the success and prayed for guidance to carry the new burden of leadership. All three of us were unusually emotional and thus established a bond of close personal friendship and understanding to 'look out' for each other and to be 'each others keeper'.

> Today, we have a new opportunity as a nation to collectively and individually work together to take this country forward, to develop and transform Sierra Leone that we all can be proud of. . . . . As we celebrate 57th years of our independence we have to acknowledge the fact that as a country we are at a crossroad and that we are faced with the stark choice between the corrupt and indisciplined business as usual status quo or a change to a new direction where every Sierra Leonean is given the ladder of opportunity to climb and achieve their greatest potential . . . .We have to ask ourselves that after 57 years of independence what do we have to show for? . . . . After 57 years of political independence, we are still faced with some of the most critical problems and challenges of development and social progress. . . .My Government will only fund future independence celebrations across the country when, as a nation, we are able to pay for our critical and basic services without relying on any external development aid. My Government will only approve future funding for independence celebration activities when our domestic revenue collection makes up 20% of our Gross Domestic Product [31]

Similarly, in the inaugural address by the newly elected President Bio to the nation delivered on 12th May 2018 at the Saika Stevens Stadium, the speech importantly stressed, 'We now have the unique opportunity to develop and implement a new Development Plan for Sierra Leone. . . . My government is therefore launching three peaceful democratic wars. First, a war on indiscipline. Second, a war on Corruption, and Third, a War on Poverty. These peaceful democratic wars on indiscipline, corruption and poverty will define my tenure of office. . . I will provide the discipline leadership to drive and sustain our new direction revolution. . . . .My government will tirelessly work for and remain committed to inclusive politics, inclusive development, inclusive economic growth, and inclusive governance.'[32]

Perhaps the most memorable speech written would be remembered not because of its impact but simply for how we were taken advantage of as a new administration. I wrote the speech for the president, which he delivered at the side event of the London CHOGM Summit on 18th

---

[31] State House Press Secretary, '57th Independence Anniversary Address to the Nation by His Excellency President Julius Maada Bio, 27th April 2019, Siaka Stevens National Stadium.

[32] State House Press Secretary, Inaugural Address by His Excellency President Julius Maada Bio at Saika Stevens Stadium on 12th May 2018.

April 2018, at which President Bio committed the Government of Sierra Leone to a new global goal of achieving 12 years of quality education for all girls by 2030. The side event was organised by the Commonwealth Women's Fund on the theme 'Towards a Common Future: An Empowered Future for Women and Girls'. In the run-up to the participation of the newly elected president at the CHOGM Summit, I was inundated with meetings with the British High Commissioner, Guy Warrington, and the DFID Country Manager, Mary Hunt, who specifically requested that President Bio make a national commitment to deliver 12 years of girl child education. They even provided the forms of words for the speech and both assured that if President Bio makes this commitment, the UK government will release a total of £24 million, paid in two tranches, to support the education programmes of the new administration in Sierra Leone. President Bio welcomed this early indication of support and prospect to fund the Free Education programme of the New Direction administration. In the speech, I made sure that President Bio made the public commitment, stating that, 'I, therefore, commit my new government to deliver 12 years of good quality education by 2030. I commit to ensuring that girls, children with disability, and other disadvantage groups have equal opportunities to complete the full cycle of primary and secondary education. I am making this Commitment to Action because I firmly believe that free education is the bedrock for sustainable development and long-term peace. By this action, we are fulfilling the UN Sustainable Development Goal 4. . . .'[33]

To cut a long story short, we, as a government, only received the promised £24 million three years later, even though we were reliably informed, based on informal and confidential discussions with senior UK-FCO and DFID officers in London, that the UK government had released the grant. In fact, when the Office of the President made a follow-up on the release of the funds to support the start of the Free Quality Education programme, the British High Commission and DFID officers told us that it was too expensive and unaffordable to roll out a national programme of free education; as such, we should not be focusing on such an agenda as a new administration. This was the same negative response to the free education agenda from our Western diplomatic and development partners. It was only when President Bio

[33] State House Press Secretary, 'President Bio Commits to 2030 Education Goal for Girls', 18th April 2018.

took the bold, if not audacious, step to finance the start and implementation of the Free Quality Education in August 2018 that the UK and other Western diplomatic partners, including the international financial institutions such as the IMF and the World Bank, all showed willingness to support the government's new Free Quality Education programme.[34] At the time of writing this book, the then Minister of Basic and Senior Secondary Education, Alpha Timbo, whose outstanding leadership of the newly created Ministry, was responsible for the successful implementation of the New Direction Government's Free Quality Education programme. It was the strategic and high-level intervention of Minister Alpha Timbo that led to the release of the £24 million UK-DfID grant to support diverse education programme interventions in Sierra Leone[35].

Chairman of Governance Transition Team: aspiration to set an anti-corruption agenda

The first task of the newly sworn-in president was to convene a high-level advisory meeting comprising senior advisers and party leaders on 5th April 2018 at the Radisson Blu Hotel. The outcome of this high-level meeting was the establishment of a board-based Governance Transition Team (GTT), the membership of which was personally nominated by President Bio, who rejected any nomination by the close advisers attempting to bring onboard 'neo-patrimonial 'friends and allies'. I was appointed by the president to chair and effectively progress the work of the GTT within a 3-month mandate. The primary purpose of the GTT was to conduct an 'immediate stocktaking of the state of affairs of Government Ministries, Departments, and Agencies (MDAs) and to submit a report to the President and Vice President on its findings'.[36]

After much national anticipation and media speculation, I presented, on behalf of the team, the GTT Report to His Excellency President Bio at State House on 4th July 2018. The President used the opportunity to

[34] As Chief Minister, I later served as Co-Chair for the GoSL – Development Partners FQE Implementation Committee.

[35] The funds were released based on the efforts of Minister Timbo who secured the high-level visit to Sierra Leone and the diplomatic intervention of Madam Alice Albringt, the CEO of the Global Partnership for Education. Madam Albringt had earlier served as the CEO of the US-MCC from 2022 – 2025.

[36] Terms of Reference for the Governance Transition Team, 5th April 2018, p.1.

restate his commitment to the fight against corruption, stressing that 'corruption is not only a governance issue but also a national security threat'. With the formal submission of the GTT Report, President Bio convened an emergency cabinet meeting on 6th July 2018 for consideration and approval.

The GTT Report was approved by the Cabinet and the general public was duly informed thus:

1. That the Cabinet, as the highest decision-making body of the government, has endorsed the Report of the GTT 2018, approved the Recommendations of the Report, and authorised the Chief Minister, in consultation with the Attorney General and Minister of Justice, to lead the implementation of the recommendations of the Report in a timely manner.
2. That His Excellency the President has directed the Attorney General to immediately lead on the establishment of a judge-led Commission of Inquiry as provided for in Section 147 of Act No. 6 on the 1991 Constitution. The Commission will consist of a Chairman who will be a judge of international repute and other renowned judges of national repute.[37]

The GTT Report was a comprehensive audit that laid bare the scale and depth of the governance failures, problems, and challenges left behind by the APC Ernest Koroma-led government at the time of the assumption of office in April 2018. Using dispassionate academic language and some would say colourful language, such as 'egregious corruption' and 'organised criminal racketeering enterprise', the GTT report stated that the 11-year rule of President Ernest Koroma's APC administration led to rampant corruption and gross mismanagement of the state to the extent that Sierra Leone was internationally branded as the 'most corrupt country in the world'. The report cataloged the scale of the economic crisis bequeathed to the new SLPP government led by President Bio, stating that the country faced near-economic collapse due to fiscal indiscipline and rampant corrupt; high burden liabilities amounting to USD $3.7 billion as at March 2018; massive and unsustainable debt burden with USD $1.6 billion in external debt, USD $658 million in domestic debt and a large USD $1.4 billion owed to vendors for goods and services; bloated government payroll about USD

[37] State House Press Secretary, 'Update on the GTT Report: Next Steps', 9th July 2018.

$263 million, i.e., 14.4% of GDP; depreciated and severally devalued national currency trading at Le7,600 to a dollar, and significant reduction in economic growth from 6% in 2016 to 3.7% in 2017. Based on the extent of the findings, the Report made 10 key recommendations, including to 'immediately institute a Judge-led Special Commission of Inquiry…to recover all stolen or inappropriately converted state funds and other assets…They should recommend for prosecution former APC officials whose corrupt conduct is found to be particularly egregious.'[38]

The GTT Report was explosive and political dynamite because it openly and audaciously presented for public scrutiny the scale and depth of the pervasive and rampant corruption that had plagued the nation since the attainment of political independence. The report became a divisive and controversial political issue in the country at that time. Three important developments unfolded.

First, I suddenly became a national figure and household name, praised and vilified in equal measure, depending on which political party one belonged to or the rational view of governance as pertaining to the efficient political and economic management of the state and its resources.

Second, I was immediately subjected to political intimidation and harassment, with persistent death threats, which warranted the provision of combined OSD and military personnel as bodyguards and close protection officers. I found all of these amusing and realised that it was a deliberate ploy to intimidate me to the point that I become frightened and return back to England to my quiet and dignified academic life and secure environment. Obviously, I never allowed the detractors to win and even aggressively took the 'hostility' and 'political battle' to them, which forced them to relent, and in the process, I acquired a grudging respect as a 'tough guy' and one not to be messed with.

Third, the GTT Report was covertly used and misused by those who felt aggrieved by the APC administration to settle old scores and go after their perceived 'enemies'. Without my knowledge and approval

[38] Office of the President, Government of Sierra Leone, Report of the Governance Transition Team 2018. The GTT members included: Professor David J. Francis (Chairman); Dr. Abass C. Bundu; Dr. Morie Manyeh; Mrs Kona Koroma; Mr Jacob Jusu Saffa; Alhaji Kanja Sesay; Dr Alie Kabba; PC Charles Caulker: Mr Umaru Koroma; Mr Denis Vandy; Ms Melrose Kargbo; Mr. Sahr Jusu; Hon Suahilo Koroma and Dr Dennis Sandy (Secretary).

as Chairman of GTT and newly appointed as Chief Minister, these aggrieved persons 'announced' that all those mentioned in the GTT report, whether as government ministers or private sector business owners, had their bank accounts frozen and needed clearance from the office of the president and chief minister for all international travel. This was never authorised and sanctioned by the president, vice president or chief minister. The GTT Report itself never recommended the action of freezing bank accounts and banning travel. In effect, at the time of my appointment as chief minister, I had already become a polarising public figure, unwittingly 'hated' not because of actions personally taken, but largely due to misplaced political perceptions and the attribution of actions to the GTT Chairman, which were unfounded. To a very large extent, this was my 'baptism of political fire' and harsh introduction into the brutal, manipulative, and ruthless world of the nature of domestic politics in Sierra Leone.

Mandate and Functions of the Chief Minister: From Improvisation to Policy-Practice Fait

In assuming the challenging responsibility to effectively govern the country, President Bio was aware that the New Direction administration needed a strong coordinating, monitoring, supervisory, and performance management hub at the heart of the administration to drive the implementation of service delivery for the people of the country. Bearing in mind, the people had voted for change in government and they expected immediate results and outcomes.

While at the University of Bradford, both the President and I informally brainstormed and developed strategies on how to make governance deliver for the people, by creating a new governance structure to support the executive functions of both the president and vice president.

Additionally, the President was very clear that his governance approach would be different and progressive because he was aware that every 'little' and inconsequential matter was often directed to the Presidency or Office of the President, thereby overwhelming the delivery capacity of the President. As such, an important rationale for the appointment of the Chief Minister was to 'free up the valuable time' of the President, to enable him to focus on important policy and strategic development decision-making issues. The State House Press

Secretary stated on 1st May 2018 that the appointment of the Chief Minister by the President was primarily motivated by the efforts to ensure that the new government delivered on the key strategic priorities. On my appointment, I empathically stated that 'My office works as the coordinating link at the ministerial level with all ministries but also at the cabinet level and the day-to-day operational level with the Office of the Secretary to the President. This is the place where we coordinate and push the implementation of government programmes from the centre. For this country and the New Direction to succeed it needs a strong Presidency, strong centre. This is why the Office of the Chief Minister was constituted. Colleagues who have served as ministers before are saying that they are very pleased that the president appointed a chief minister because we have somebody who follows up and coordinates the implementation at all levels of government'[39].

To this end, the six principal functions of the Chief Minister were

1. Principal Advisory Role
2. Supervisory, Coordination, Follow-Up, and Monitoring Functions
3. Performance Management across Ministries, Departments, and Agencies (MDAs) for Results-Based Service Delivery
4. Policy, planning, and strategy role for development of key governance institutions
5. Chairing Inter-Ministerial Thematic and Sector Committees
6. Special Envoy Missions

I have to state from the onset that when President Bio appointed me as chief minister, there was no job description, terms of reference, or job specification outlining the roles, functions, and mandate of the Chief Minister and the Office of the Chief Minister. As pointed out earlier, this was the first such appointment in the Republic of Sierra Leone since the 1971 Republican Constitution, which abolished the parliamentary system of government in favour of a presidential system.

To all intents and purposes, I stood up and established the roles, functions, and mandate of the Chief Minister and Office of the Chief Minister, making sure that the mandate and functions do not in any way clash with or duplicate the mandate of the vice president as provided for

[39] Statement by Chief Minister Professor David Francis, State House, 8th May 2018.

in Section 54 of the 1991 Constitution or attempt to diminish any of the functions, mandate, and powers of the executive authority and powers of the executive residency as stipulated in Section 53.

It was not a simple recreation of the British colonial administration's Chief Minister, nor the modern-day Federalist countries that have regional states headed by constitution that describe them as chief ministers. The New Direction establishment of the post of Chief Minister as a senior Cabinet Minister was a new governance, administrative, and political structure deliberately crafted to make governance efficient and to lead on the delivery of outcomes/results-based services for the people of Sierra Leone. Under the President's and the Vice President's monitoring and guidance, I was given a free hand and political support, backed by the President's authority and power, to establish and operationalise the role and mandate of the Chief Minister and that of the Office of the Chief Minister.

In fact, a major problem with the assumption of the Office of the Chief Minister was that I immediately assumed responsibility for the programmes and staff of the defunct Office of the Chief of Staff in the Office of the President. Based on an internal administrative audit, I found that the 105 staff employed in the Office of the Chief of Staff had officers who were also receiving salaries from externally funded projects, and most of the staff did not have job specifications. Taking the advice of the senior Permanent Secretary in the Office of the Chief Minister, the 105 staff were rationalised and only 5 administrative and support staff were retained. To implement a governance and administrative process that valued a lean, competence-based, professional, and efficient administration in the Office of the Chief Minister, we recruited 12 competent professional staff to support the work of the Office of the Chief Minister.

As Chief Minister, I assumed responsibility for the diverse functions and service delivery programmes that had formerly resided within the Office of the Chief of Staff. I realised that this was a recipe for ineffectiveness because I could not possibly deliver on all the prescribed mandates of the Chief Minister whilst at the same time taking on residual responsibilities from the defunct Office of the Chief of Staff. To this end, I advised the President, and he approved that the US-funded Millennium Challenge Corporation (MCC) project, previously managed by the Office of the Chief of Staff, be delegated to the Vice President and the Office of the Vice President to serve as the lead GoSL agency on all matters pertinent to the successful preparation and winning of the MCC grant.

The bold leadership in transferring the delivery of the MCC project to the Office of the Vice President generated its own 'internal' controversy because some 'well-meaning' Cabinet colleagues quietly raised their concerns to me that it was ill-advised to move the MCC project to the Office of the Vice President since no one in government voluntarily gives power away to another colleague or agency of government, with all the access to resources that goes with such donor-funded projects. I was confident that this was the right decision to advise the President and secured his approval for me to transfer the MCC project to the leadership of the Vice President, Dr Mohamed Juldeh Jalloh. With the benefit of hindsight, I now realise that this was an inspired decision because Vice President Juldeh Jalloh provided impressive leadership in managing and successfully securing the MCC grant of a USD $480 million compact agreement for GoSL in September 2024.

Nevertheless, there was a 'politically' motivated effort to create confusion and to misrepresent the role and mandate of the Chief Minister, deliberately claiming that the role overlapped, duplicated, and clashed with the constitutional functions of the Vice President. This was certainly not the case because the constitutional role/functions and mandate of the Vice President are clearly stipulated in Section 54 of the 1991 Constitution. Addressing the media controversy sparked by my appointment, I categorically stated that: 'The Vice President is the principal assistant to the president. The role of the chief minister is not even in the Constitution. It is a presidential prerogative. My role as chief minister is to support the president and vice president in the delivery of their executive functions'.[40]

[40] State House Press Briefing on the Role and Mandate of the Chief Minister, 9th May 2018.

CHAPTER THREE

Presidential Advisory, Governance Delivery Retreats, and Ministerial Performance Management Role of Chief Minister

Introduction

Across the country, there is a general lack of understanding among the citizens about the functions and mandate of the Chief Minister as a 'new' governance structure, including the so-called traditional politicians. As such, this lack of clear understanding of the roles and responsibilities of the Chief Minister in modern Sierra Leone, where the governance architecture is based on a unitary state with an executive presidential system, has led to misconceptions, misrepresentations, and controversies about the role and mandate of the Chief Minister. Chapter 3 therefore provides practical evidence of the roles and responsibilities of the Chief Minister as appointed by the New Direction administration of President Bio. The chapter assesses the key roles and mandate of the chief minister as the principal senior minister responsible for the supervision, coordination and follow-up, performance management, and monitoring of the 28 New Direction GoSL ministries and 14 legislated agencies within the Office of the President. Chapter 3 outlines and evaluates the key governance delivery roles and responsibilities of the Chief Minister including; serving as one of the Principal Advisers to the President and how this produced the Presidential Executive Order No. 1; leading on the organisation and facilitation of the Cabinet/Ministerial Retreats as well as the political and administrative interface retreat/seminars for Civil Servants/Permanent Secretaries, Parliamentarians, Commissions, State Owned Enterprises and Parastatals; the organisation and delivery of Ministerial Performance Management and Contract; governance coordination and follow-up role through Inter-Ministerial Committees on cross-cutting and sectoral issues to support effective service delivery.

Principal Advisory Role and Presidential Executive Orders

To fully appreciate the extent of the practical and operational role and mandate of the Chief Minister, it is important to start with the presidential advisory role because all directives and authority to act or undertake any particular governance-related work, venture, or assignment are derived from, assigned, or delegated by the President and the President alone. Let me illustrate the importance of this presidential advisory role. As Chairman of the GTT and based on extensive consultations with President Bio, and in collaboration with the Office of the Secretary to the President, I drafted four key items as Executive Orders, relating to the effective political and economic management of the State, which the President approved. On 9th April 2018, the Office of the President issued Executive Order No. 1, an immediate directive designed for swift action and implementation across Sierra Leone. The Executive Order No1 stated:

1. All public sector workers and government ministers are required to be in office from 8:30am till 4:45pm. The President and Vice President will conduct routine and unannounced checks at Ministries, Departments, and Agencies (MDAs) to ensure implementation. Failure to report to work on time will lead to disciplinary action and potential summary dismissal.
2. A National Cleaning Day is declared for the first Saturday of each month from 7:00am to 12:00 noon. The first National Cleaning Day scheduled by the Ministry of Health and Sanitation Affairs is Saturday, 5th May 2018.
3. Re-introduce Sunday trading and commercial activities effective Sunday, 15th April 2018. The public is notified that all businesses, trading and commercial enterprises, and activities are now permitted to operate on Sundays, only between the periods of 12:00 and 5:00pm
4. All Ministries, Departments, and Agencies (MDAs) and other public sector institutions are now required to host all government-related workshops, seminars, and conferences at MDAs/Public Sector Institution premises and not at hotels. The objective is to save cost and prevent wastage of scarce government resources.[1]

Presidential Executive Order No. 1 was immediately followed by Executive Order No. 2, which was championed by the Ministry of Finance as a manifesto commitment. Presidential Executive Order No.

[1] State House Press Secretary, Executive Order No 1. Freetown, 9th April 2018.

2 focused on the implementation of a Government of Sierra Leone Single Treasury Account (STA) on revenue mobilisation, requiring all MDAs that collect and retain government revenue to transfer all such revenues into the Consolidated Revenue Fund (CRF) in line with the provisions of the Fiscal Management and Control Act 2017.[2]

Both Presidential Executive Orders were driven by the simple governance imperative of the new government to be seen to act and act decisively by taking bold actions that will have an immediate, visible, and tangible impact on the lives of the people, who now expected so much from a new government that they voted for on the mandate for 'Change'. In advising President Bio, I argued that making sure that civil servants and public sector workers are punctual at work; 're-introduction' of a National Cleaning Day; the re-introduction of Sunday trading and commercial activities; and requiring MDAs to host workshops, seminars, and conferences at their premises were regarded as governance low-hanging fruits and quick wins for the new administration. By all indications, these populist presidential executive orders were widely applauded by the citizens who perceived the new government as being on the side of the people and one that meant a complete change in the indisciplined and ineffective governance status quo.

Though these presidential executive orders made the President and the New Direction government look very good in the eyes of the people and perceived as a breath of fresh air in governance, we nonetheless had 'spectacular' challenges in the implementation of some of these presidential executive orders. In the first place, we did not plan enough, in terms of resources and logistics, to roll out a National Cleaning Day. In my earlier discussions with President Bio on the importance of National Cleaning Day, drawing from his NPRC military rule days and the problems they encountered in rolling out a National Cleaning Day, he was astute in immediately raising concerns about the need to properly plan and prepare for the implementation of the National Cleaning Day, especially the necessity to secure reliable and readily available logistics such as heavy trucks, bulldozers, excavators, tipper/dump trucks, and general cleaning logistics. To this end, and due to the fact that the new government ministers had not yet been appointed and assumed

---

[2] Mr. Jacob JusuSaffa, a close and trusted Presidential Adviser, was the brain behind the drafting and announcement of Presidential Executive Order No 2.

responsibilities, the National Cleaning Day was initially coordinated by the Office of the President, the Ministry of Health and Sanitation, and the Ministry of Finance, as well as massive goodwill support from the private sector, especially construction companies.

Despite the initial problems and challenges in the implementation of the National Cleaning Day, it was on the whole a relatively successful effort by the New Direction administration to keep the capital city, Freetown, and the rest of the country clean as well as improve the health and wellbeing of the populace. The youth were massively mobilised across the country and in Freetown, with government officers, including the president and first lady, taking active part in the First-Saturday, National Cleaning Day activities. In Freetown, the National Cleaning Day drastically reduced the incidents of flooding due to the regular cleaning and maintenance of the drainage systems and gutters.

Notwithstanding, the National Cleaning Day implementation was later supervised and monitored by the Ministry of Youth Affairs and the Ministry of Local Government and Rural Development, with funding from the Ministry of Finance. As always, the negative impact of the neo-patrimonial nature of domestic politics in Sierra Leone eventually 'usurped' and subverted the effective implementation of the National Cleaning Day. For a start, the Mayor of the Freetown City Council (FCC), Yvonne Aki Swayer, from the opposition APC Party, used every opportunity to complain to our international development partners that the National Cleaning Day was a usurpation of the functions of her FCC administration, although the other 21 local councils across the country effectively cooperated with the central government to manage the implementation of the National Cleaning Day activities.

As such, the politicisation of the National Cleaning Day undermined the efficacy and relevance of the National Cleaning Day. What is more, the National Cleaning Day exercise became a new source for corrupt practices and 'money-making', as the same logistical items were budgeted every month, though the cleaning items were only used for one day, such as shovels, cutlasses, heavy-duty gloves, trash pickers, and heavy-duty boots. Despite the rather popular appeal of the National Cleaning Day, it was suspended by the Office of the President because of the outbreak of the COVID-19 pandemic in the country in March 2020.

The widespread popular support generated by these Executive Orders served to bolster the New Direction administration's governance credentials. This public resonance provided the political capital necessary to validate President Bio's early delivery agenda. However, the negative, if not entrenched, nature of the domestic politics literarily 'kills' and undermines the implementation of every well-meaning and good-intentioned governance agenda and programme. As a government, in particular, the Office of the President and the Chief Minister were not able to persistently and consistently monitor the effective implementation of the executive orders. The're-introduction' of Sunday trading and commercial activities[3], had not been effectively monitored by the Ministry of Trade and Industry and the Office of the Chief Minister. Notwithstanding, the reintroduction of Sunday trading and commercial activities was widely and popularly received by the citizens, irrespective of the party-political divide, and immediately contributed to boosting the economy and increasing tax revenue across the country.

However, the re-introduction of Sunday trading, according to the Executive Order directive, the Sunday trading and commercial activities were required to commence from 12:00 – 5:00pm, but now they have become a 'free for all', a kind of informal 'laissez-faire' operations, starting at 9:00am till 12:00 mid-night and beyond.

The hosting of workshops, seminars and conferences at MDAs premises have also not been effectively implemented as a cost-saving governance directive. Within these MDAs, special-interest groups and individuals who have long-standing arrangements with hotels to secure private commissions not only quietly resisted the implementation of this Executive Order but also lobbied external partners funding such events to insist on hosting MDA workshops, seminars, and conferences at hotels so that they can secure their 'private commissions'.

What the Chief Minister Does in Practice?

Beyond the glamour and prestige of the Office of the Chief Minister, the populace and even those in governance, seem to have a rather vague idea or notion of what the Chief Minister actually does on a day-to-day basis. Let me be unambiguously clear, the role of the Chief Minister and the Office of the Chief Minister, as designed, assigned and delegated by

---

[3] Sunday trading and commercial activities was banned by the Ernest Koroma APC government due to the outbreak of the Ebola epidemic in Sierra Leone and the tri-states of Guinea and Liberia in 2014.

President Bio, was to serve and operate as a senior minister, in terms of being the *primus inter pares*, i.e., regarded as the 'First among Equals' of Ministers appointed by the President as per sections 40, 53 and 56 of the 1991 Constitution, also colloquially described by Cabinet colleagues as 'the Senior Prefect' of Ministers.

In terms of the Constitutional Order of Ministerial precedence, the Chief Minister is the fourth in rank, after the Executive President, Executive Vice President, and Speaker of Parliament. While in terms of the Executive Ministerial Order of Precedence, the Chief Minister is the third in cabinet rank after the President and Vice President. Even the seating arrangements at Cabinet meetings are organised in terms of protocols, with the Chief Minister always seated next to or behind the Vice President.

To get a sense of what the Chief Minister actually does and regarded as one of the important functions, was to attend, seat-in, and participate in governance-related meetings, internal / national and international delegation meetings, Presidential Briefings and Diplomatic relations meetings with the President. These meetings, mostly chaired by the President, includes the Weekly Presidential Security briefing[4]; the monthly Economic Management Team and Cabinet meetings; National Defence Council; National Security Council; Presidential COVID 19 Task Force, Parliamentarians, the Judiciary, sector MDAs, and a variety of specific and generic governance-related high-level meetings. These diverse meetings would go on for a whole day, from 9:00am – 6:00pm,

[4] As Chief Minister, I introduced the governance practice of a Weekly Presidential Security Briefing at 10:00am on Mondays, by the Security Sector including the heads of the RSLAF; SL Police, National Security Coordinator of the Office of the National Security (ONS); Head of the Fire Force / Brigade; the National Security Adviser; CISU etc as well as the President, the Vice President, the Chief Minister, Finance Minister, AGMoJ and Secretary to the President. On assumption of the governance, President Bio inherited an ad hoc and on a needs-basis, security briefing on the state of affairs of the security situations in the country, transnational crimes and external security threats. Given the importance of the security sector and situation in the country on peace, stability and development of the state, President Bio accepted my recommendation for immediate implementation the governance format of Weekly Presidential Security Briefing as a practical effort to know what is happening in the security landscape of the country on a weekly and daily basis. Though this security briefing format, I developed an excellent, cordial and respectful working relationship with the security sector.

often with no time to reflect or thoroughly read the prepared pre-meeting briefs.

A major component of my attendance or participation in these meetings was the 'follow-up' on decisions made for action or the delegation to the appropriate head of MDAs, the 'follow-up' for action. Typically, at the end of each day, I often had a long list of presidential decisions that I had to follow up on or ensure coordination of the sector MDAs to facilitate implementation and to assess the impact of the results or outcomes.

Additionally, as Chief Minister and with the support of the SCOP, it was my responsibility to brief the President on each of these meetings, stating their relevance and who or which personality was leading the delegation, so that the President can address such heads of delegation with or in their specific honorific titles. The participation or seating-in on all high-level Presidential meetings and follow-up on governance-related decisions were a major part of the role and day-to-day operational mandate of the Chief Minister. These diverse, multi-sectoral Presidential meetings are not merely ceremonial; they reside at the very heart of the state's architecture, serving as the primary engine for governance delivery to the people.

As Chief Minister, I chaired, on behalf of the President or Vice President, several inter-ministerial committees and the formal launch of government programmes that the President or Vice President were not able to attend. An illustrative example was that as Chief Minister, I chaired the event that formally launched the Free Quality School Education Programme on 20th August 2018 at the Maitta Conference Hall, at which, both the President and Vice President were in attendance. Another illustrative example was on 16th September 2019 when President Bio directed that as Chief Minister, I use my academic and intellectual background to build an 'Education Coalition', bringing together retired eminent educationists to dialogue and develop framework on the future of education in Sierra Leone against the background of the introduction of Free Quality School Education reform agenda. I convened at State House the first such high-level meeting which recommended strategies on how to address the inherited menace of public education exams malpractice that was rampant across the education sector. As always, such good intentioned Presidential initiative was not sustained because the eminent members of the 'Coalition for Education' gradually lost interest because of lack of remuneration for the services rendered. The Ministry of Basic Education also raised concerns that this 'advisory group' may well encroach on their strategic policy domain.

However, this was not the first disappointment with educationists in the country. Following the launch of the Free Quality Education initiative, President Bio mandated the Office of the Chief Minister to convene the leadership of the higher education sector. This engagement was designed to broaden the 'Coalition for Education,' ensuring that the national educational strategy remained integrated and sustainable. The strategic thinking on this matter was very clear in that, as a new government, we realised that it was one thing to roll-out Free Education at Primary and Secondary School levels, but the important consideration was what happened when the mass of post-Secondary students leave school. Without doubt, these post-secondary school students needed university placements and access to technical and vocational training centres.

To this end, I convened a high-level meeting at State House for all the public higher education leadership including the Ministers of Basic Education and the Minister of Technical and Higher Education (MoTHE), chaired by the President. The meeting produced very positive outcomes including the commitment to produce a blueprint and roadmap on the Future of Education in Sierra Leone and the imperative to establish new public Universities to accommodate the post-Secondary School educational needs of Sierra Leoneans. Again, the leadership of the public higher education institutions disappointed the President by failing to develop and submit the promised 'Roadmap on the Future of Education'.

Notwithstanding the initial challenges, this engagement yielded a significant outcome: it catalysed the process for establishing three new public universities. This expansion was subsequently spearheaded by the MoTHE as a core component of the Government's Human Capital Development strategy. As Chief Minister and as an established academic, I supported the Ministers of MoTHE, Professor AiahGbakima and Professor Alpha Wurie, to process the legislative approval for the establishment of the three new universities in the form of the new Universities Act 2021, replacing the 2005 Universities Act, and the formal establishment of the three new universities including the Eastern Technical University in Kenema; Milton Margai Technical University and the Kono University of Science and Technology.

Additionally, as Chief Minister and with the support of the Office of the Chief Minister, I chaired and organised all three Cabinet Retreats and the medium-term evaluation of the government as well as retreat for heads of government MDA, state owned enterprises, parastatals, and permanent secretaries between 2018 and 2020.

The construction of the role and mandate of chief minister as a senior minister or 'senior prefect' of minister ensured that the president often appointed the chief minister as acting minister in the absence of the substantive minister. One such occasion was when President Bio appointed me to serve as Acting Minister of Foreign Affairs and International Cooperation on 28th June 2018, when the substantive minister, Dr Alie Kabba, had to attend the ECOWAS Executive Council Meeting. In taking my Oath of Office as Acting Minister to the President, I stated, 'I, Professor David John Francis, do hereby, in the name of God, swear that I will faithfully and truly discharge the duties of the Office of Acting Minister of the Ministry of Foreign Affairs and International Cooperation of the Republic of Sierra Leone, and that I will support, uphold, and maintain the Constitution as by law established'.[5]

The governance practice of a senior minister serving in an acting capacity in the absence of the substantive officeholder is not new to Sierra Leone. In Ghana and Liberia, where there is an established governance practice of 'Senior Minister', the Senior Minister is automatically appointed as Acting Minister in the absence of the substantive office holder. In most governance situations across the world, this is the standard practice and expectation. In my case, however, the pattern shifted. My tenure as Acting Foreign Minister proved to be my final such assignment, as the President thereafter moved away from appointing me to temporary roles in the absence of substantive office holders. I was 'informed' that some of the 'close allies' and 'self-appointed gatekeepers' of the President complained that President Bio was making the Chief Minister 'too powerful'. These 'complainants' seemed unable to reconcile themselves to a fundamental reality: that our reforms were rooted in institutional governance and standardised procedure, rather than being directed at any specific individual. To them and from the embedded negative nature of the domestic politics

---

[5] Office of the President, State House, Freetown, Sierra Leone, 'Oath of Office as Acting Minister of Foreign Affairs and International Cooperation', 28th June 2018.

perspective, it was bad for the president to appoint the chief minister because it potentially made the chief minister 'too powerful'. Yet, these same 'close allies' and 'complainants', when appointed to acting roles, despite their substantive offices, did not claim or complain that it made them 'too powerful'. The important governance delivery point that I am making is that the negative nature of domestic politics determined whether a government succeeded or failed, no matter how well-meaning or well-intentioned.

Service Delivery Culture in Governance: Retreats for Cabinet Ministers and Heads of MDAs, Civil Service – Political Leadership Interface

The public announcement of the 28 Cabinet Ministers, State Ministers, and Resident Ministers was appreciated by the citizens. The general view was that the new Cabinet team inspired national and international confidence in terms of the caliber, competence, maturity, experience and professionalism of the ministerial appointments. Some of the newly appointed Cabinet Ministers had significant governance backgrounds, international leadership exposure, and demonstrable leadership track records because some had been former ministers and heads of government agencies in the previous SLPP government of President Kabbah and the APC administration of President Koroma. However, the majority had limited governance and public sector leadership experience. In effect, the first problem of the new administration of President Bio was how to encourage and motivate a high-performing, competent, professional, and disciplined leadership team. To achieve this governance imperative, I proposed to President Bio the concept and practice of a Cabinet Retreat to achieve the much-needed governance service delivery and team-building strategic objectives.[6] President Bio approved the proposal of a Cabinet Retreat for the new administration and directed the Office of the Chief Minister, in collaboration with the Cabinet Secretariat, to lead on the organisation of the approved Cabinet Retreat.

---

[6] In the run-up to the Presidential Elections in 2018, one of the tasks designated to me by the Presidential Candidate, Julius Maada Bio, was to, among other responsibilities, develop a New Direction 100 Days Plan of Action for Quick-impact governance interventions. As such, the proposed Cabinet Retreat and the Executive Orders No. 1 & 2, were all part of the 100 Days Plan.

Based on the above, what then is the purpose of governance retreats? In general, governance retreats serve the purpose to provide reflective, cordial and professional space to candidly agree on and set realistic priorities and targets based on SMART (Specific, Measurable, Achievable, Realistic, and Timebound) for service delivery as well as to assess and review service delivery results, outcomes, and impact. Governance retreats are used to brainstorm, through a problem-solving and 'can do' approach, to identify gaps, limitations, problems, and challenges in service delivery. It provides the unique opportunity to develop a common understanding and appreciation of how to manage the citizens' service delivery expectations and appreciate that the implementation of service delivery is hard work, not a quick fix often with fluctuations, highs and lows, between setting and achieving goals. A key purpose of a governance retreat is that it is a platform to build and encourage a high-performing team spirit with a sense of collective responsibility. It has become a framework to establish a service delivery way of working, a delivery routine, a delivery culture, and a delivery mentality, thereby creating the discipline of service delivery. What is important about the governance retreat is that it brings about a shift from a government approach that prioritises governance improvisation, ad hoc activities, soundbites, hyperactivity, massaged messages and press releases, and crisis management where everything matters and the government is remote or far removed from the people and often slow in action to a government by routine with clear priorities, specification of successes, routine oversight, and government informed by real-time data and research-based evidence to inform policy, planning, and strategy.

Governance Retreat has become a forum that is open to dialogue, able and willing to accept mistakes and failures, but at the same time focused on the future and persistent in the drive to achieve concrete and tangible results and outcomes on the ground for the benefit of the people. If anything, the governance retreat has become a platform for effective interface, collaboration, and cordial working relationships between ministers, heads of government departments and agencies and civil servants. The principles underpinning the purpose of governance retreats includes, agenda setting, performance review, accountability and recalibration, and service delivery focus.

With this in mind and as Chief Minister, in collaboration with the Cabinet Secretariat, I led the organisation of the following Cabinet / Ministerial retreats between 2018 and 2020:

1. First Cabinet/Ministerial Retreat on 22-23 June 2018.
2. Second Cabinet/Ministerial Retreat on 10-11 January 2019
3. Medium-Term Evaluation of the New Direction Government on 12 October 2020
4. Presidential Retreat for GoSL Commissions/Parastatals/Agencies and State-Owned Enterprises on 23 May 2020

On my appointment as Chief Minister, one of my first governance delivery task was to facilitate and organise the first Cabinet Retreat in June 2018, just three months after the SLPP and President Bio assumed leadership of the country. As a new administration, I was aware that the SLPP manifesto made too many promises, some unrealistic to be achieved within a five-year mandate and electoral cycle. I was also aware that President Bio was elected on the ticket and mandate for 'change' and as such, the citizens expected more from the New Direction administration and immediately. As Chief Minister, I had to manage pressures from two fronts. I assisted the President in navigating public expectations, while clarifying to Cabinet colleagues that the Chief Minister is a facilitator of the governance process, not a singular source of all delivery answers. To this end, the First Cabinet Retreat was also an agenda-setting opportunity to encourage and promote the development of a spirit of collective ownership and responsibility, a 'we are all in this together', but at the same time highlighting the reputational risk of failure, hence the reminder to Cabinet colleagues, 'If I go down, we all go down'.

To deliver on this presidential initiative and approval, I mobilised my international governance networks to secure the participation of international resource persons to lead and facilitate, such as Sir Michael Barber of Delivery Associates and the then UNSRSG, Dr Mohamed Ibn Chambas. The Office of the Chief Minister also secured external funding from UNDP and DFID – Sierra Leone to partly finance the Cabinet Retreat.

The strategic objectives were to set priorities to achieve change and transformation, stay focused on delivering the defined priorities, and build and motivate high-performing teams to achieve results. The retreat provided the unique opportunity for President Bio to meet in person all his newly appointed ministers, deputy ministers, state ministers and resident ministers, stating:

> As you know, I have been at the helm of state affairs before and I know that to deliver in governance we must always conduct ourselves in a professional manner. We must lead by example and I will always be there to provide you with the disciplined leadership and support. . . . We must practice team work because every sector in governance is important. We have to be together with the right mentality to deliver on our promises. . . . It is the responsibility of all Ministers to ensure the collective delivery of the promises that I have made to Sierra Leoneans. . . We now have the unique opportunity to rewrite the narrative in our history books and go down as the set of people who saved the nation. . . Let us collectively make use of this opportunity and once again make our country an enviable place to live.[7]

As Moderator Chair, I reiterated President Bio's message, stressing that the retreat 'will help us to develop a high-performing team spirit that will encourage us to collectively deliver on the hopes of Sierra Leoneans. As ministers, we will work as close friends, tied towards a clear objective – the New Direction governance agenda'. [8]

The First Cabinet Retreat achieved the difficult task of rationalising the 138 SLPP Manifesto Commitments into 8 National Priorities through a deliberative process of 'ruthless prioritisation'.[9] The 8 priorities were education, agriculture, energy, macro-economy, water and sanitation, security, health, justice and anti-corruption. The 8 priorities derived from the SLPP Manifesto were envisaged as a roadmap to deliver tangible results and outcomes. Functioning as a strategic roadmap, these eight priorities served as the foundational framework from which ministries derived specific policies. This

---

[7] State House Press Secretary, His President Bio's Address to the Cabinet Retreat on 22 June 2018.

[8] Chief Minister's Address at Cabinet Retreat, 22-23 June 2018.

[9] Michael Barber, 'How to Run a Government: So That Citizens Benefit & Taxpayers Don't Go Crazy', Penguin Books, 2015

structure ensured that sectoral strategies were intentionally designed for implementation and the measurable delivery of outcomes.[10]

Based on the 'ruthless prioritisation' process of rationalising the 138 SLPP Manifesto commitments into 8 priorities, as chief minister, I immediately realised that in the context of Sierra Leone's governance delivery, everything was a priority because of the persistent levels of underdevelopment, poor leadership, and poverty. In effect, the governance delivery challenge for any serious, sober, and well-meaning Chief Minister in the country was how to prioritise the 'priority' of what was to be done and delivered for the people. In several respects, the 'ruthless' prioritisation and rationalisation of manifesto commitments represented a profound attempt at socio-political reform. It moved the New Direction administration beyond simple performance target-setting toward a fundamental restructuring of the state's operational logic.

The Second Retreat on the theme 'Strengthening Political and Administrative Interface for Effective Service Delivery' uniquely brought together Ministers and Permanent Secretaries/Civil Servants to:

1. review progress on the rationalised 8 priorities developed from the SLPP Manifesto and identify key successes, barriers, and future actions and identify key actions to tackle strategic issues
2. build a strong collective commitment to taking the necessary action and delivery on the 8 priorities
3. develop a sound relationship between ministers and civil servants and identify areas for improving the delivery capability
4. identify and commit to the key features of an effective delivery culture.

This political and administrative interface bringing together ministers and civil servants was a very important governance delivery strategy in that there is often no 'love lust' between government ministers and permanent secretaries/civil servants. The perception and attitude of most ministers is to blame the failures and problems of governance delivery on the civil servants because of what they claim to be their slow work ethic and 'state capture' mentality. On the part of the civil servants, especially the 'politicised' elements, often deliberately undermine the

[10] These 8 National Priorities were later incorporated into the Ministry of Economic Development & Planning-led Sierra Leone's Medium-Term National Development Plan 2019 - 2023

ministers, believing that the Civil Servants have a permanent tenure while appointed ministers have a rather short-term tenure in government. Bringing the political (ministers) and administrative (permanent secretaries) leadership together was a refreshing opportunity to develop a common understanding of the New Direction government's core governance priorities, facilitate cordial understanding and good working relationships focusing on the delivery of results for the people.

The outcome of the Second Retreat identified the greatest threats to service delivery which included: weakness of governance delivery chains at every level (frontline, district, regional and national); glaring capacity and skill gaps in delivery chains across the eight priorities and which needed to be urgently addressed if service delivery were to happen; imperative to invest in high-quality capacity-building, not of a generic kind, but specifically focused on delivering each of the 8 priorities; identification of the lack of capacity in the delivery chain as the biggest single threat to delivery of the 8 priorities and to single out this challenge as the most important task for the new government.

The Medium-Term Evaluation Retreat on the theme 'Consolidating the Foundation for Service Delivery' had the following strategic objectives:

1. Review the New Direction administration's progress on the implementation of the 8 priorities from April 2018 – January 2020 and the Medium-Term National Development Plan
2. Prioritise target setting for the delivery of results and outcomes.
3. Ensure greater clarity in roles and responsibilities for Ministers, Deputy Ministers as well as administrative and professional heads of ministries.

The methodology for the Medium-Term Evaluation was to organise government MDAs into four key service delivery clusters, including transforming the economy, human capital development, improving governance, and improving infrastructure.

In my address as moderator and chair, I stressed the fact that the strategic objective and expected outcome for the retreat was to critically reflect on the successes, strengths, weaknesses, opportunities, and threats of the New Direction administration after two years in governance. To promote a more inclusive approach to leadership, I engaged veteran politicians and retired civil service heads from across the political divide. Their role was to provide critical perspectives and shared experiences, offering the participants a roadmap to bypass common leadership mistakes and administrative errors.

In his keynote address, President Bio stated:

> Let me start off by reminding all present that the year 2020 is the year of implementation, as the people of Sierra Leone are eagerly waiting to see effective and efficient service delivery, not just on paper but to be manifested in the lives of the ordinary man. . . The timing of the Retreat at the start of the year is strategic as it presents an opportunity for both the political and the administrative cadres of government to chart the way forward and to recalibrate efforts towards the New Direction Manifesto and the Medium-Term National Development Plan. . . The medium-term evaluation retreat is convened deliberately at the start of the New Year to review the Government's 21 months in office.[11]

President Bio used this medium-term evaluation to caution that he would no longer give any 'Yellow Card' for non-performance to poor-performing ministers and heads of government department and agencies. As such, the president directed the vice president and the chief minister to play a more intrusive role in MDAs that were not working together or underperforming, encouraging all participants to 'reset our compasses and recalibrate from the *'Minister Nor Dae Syndrome'* (Minister is not at the Office Syndrome) and work towards a more effective and efficient delivery through the official structures that exist within ministries, departments and agencies[12]."

A concrete outcome of the Medium-Term Evaluation Retreat was the comprehensive governance recommendation for immediate, action including:

i. The Office of the Chief Minister to include 'the evidence of inter-ministerial and intra-MDA collaboration' as one of the

[11] State House Press Secretary, 'Address by His Excellency President Julius Maada Bio at the Medium-Term Evaluation of the New Direction Government' at the Bintumani Conference Centre, on 24th January 2020.

[12] Ibid. 24th January 2020

indicators in the 2020 Ministerial Performance Management Review

ii. Rationalisation of all GoSL-subvented and legislated agencies
iii. The termination of 'bad GoSL contracts' to be completed before the end of the First quarter of 2020
iv. The processes for signing Ministerial Performance Undertakings must be expedited
v. Ministers should engage their deputy ministers on administrative and technical issues and give them a schedule of duties so that they can perform
vi. Develop and update ministerial mandates and responsibilities from which schedule of duties for both ministers and deputy ministers can be derived
vii. Develop a communication mechanism to ensure ministers give feedback to their deputies on cabinet matters
viii. Ministers as well as their Permanent Secretaries and Professional Heads, are encouraged to undertake an assessment of existing structures and modify them as necessary
ix. Budgetary planning should have a bottom-up orientation, including lower-level district development plans that will be aggregated by line ministries into their annual budget submissions to the Ministry of Finance.
x. Office of the Chief Minister is to provide a forum whereby ministers are able to assess progress in achieving the promises made in the SLPP Manifesto and the short-term deliverables in the MTNDP and design strategies for immediate implementation of critical ones that have not yet been achieved
xi. Office of the Chief Minister to provide space and opportunity for post-retreat reflection for ministers
xii. The Ministerial Committees for the IPAS to be strengthened; Permanent Secretaries to provide compilation of staff performance appraisals to their ministers
xiii. Government to establish a National Negotiating Team to engage on behalf of government
xiv. Government to consider establishing a National Policy Advisory structure
xv. Local government structures for planning, implementation and service delivery to be strengthened.
xvi. Cabinet Secretariat is to provide capacity-building enhancement for ministers induction training, code of conduct, media engagement and meeting management.

To strengthen governance delivery across government, the Office of the Chief Minister designed a specific retreat format as a presidential seminar for parliamentarians, GoSL legislated commissions, Parastatals, agencies, and State-Owned Enterprises (SOEs) and, in collaboration with the Cabinet Secretariat, organised a one-day retreat at the Bintumani International Conference Centre.

This retreat was motivated by the governance challenges across government whereby government commissions, parastatals, the SLPP parliamentarians and parliamentary leadership were often perceived by the executive leaders (president, vice president, chief minister, ministers and secretary to the president) as 'working at cross purposes', sometimes, deliberately against the interest of the New Direction administration agenda thereby creating unnecessary conflict of interest, causing confusion, misunderstanding, inadvertently undermining and hindering delivery of government agenda and potential failure. After several such frustrating incidents, President Bio directed the Office of the Chief Minister to organise a problem-solving seminar/retreat bringing all the relevant stakeholders to develop a common understanding of governance service delivery and to avoid/prevent the usurpation of executive functions by parliamentarians. The strategic objective of this seminar included:

a. To provide a forum for the two-party representatives (Cabinet and Parliament) to interact and define a common strategy to support the President's national reform agenda.
b. To deepen understanding and buy-in of SLPP Cabinet and Parliamentary representatives of the President's performance management and service delivery initiative;
c. To strengthen the political party membership support and mutual understanding, collective responsibility and accountability for delivery of the Human Capital Development priorities of GoSL for 2020.

Evidently, this was a highly appreciated governance interface between the executive and parliamentarians, commissions, SOEs and parastatals leadership. The outcome of the seminar produced the following: a coalition of like-minded party leadership at cabinet and Parliamentary levels formed around the president's national reform agenda; the rationale for ministerial performance management and the delivery of the Human Capital Development (HCD) priorities being clearly understood within the SLPP hierarchy; and consensus reached on the need for a high-performing team-building spirit between political heads and the leadership of the party in both cabinet and parliament.

Ministerial Performance Management for Service Delivery

As one of the principal advisers to the president on all matters relating to strategic and technical governance issues pertinent to statecraft, i.e., running the affairs of the state, the Office of the Chief Minister's broad mandate included not only the supervision and monitoring of the 28 GoSL Ministries[13] and the 14 legislative agencies in the Office of the President, but also the coordinating and oversight role of specialised and technical agencies established by the president, such as the Directorate for Science and Technology (DSTI) and the Office of the Presidential Infrastructural Initiative (OPII). As Chief Minister, I did not only support the establishment of DSTI, led by Dr David Sengeh as the Chief Innovation Officer, and OPII, headed by Dr John Tambi, but also championed all OPII and DSTI policy documents for Cabinet approval.

A key function of the Chief Minister and the Office of the Chief Minister was to formulate and lead on the implementation of ministerial performance to ensure service delivery. It is important to emphasise that the ministerial performance was only rolled out after the Cabinet retreats provided the opportunity to build a high-performing team spirit and identify the new government's governance priority agenda for implementation, with targets and goals to be achieved for each ministry. In the Second Cabinet Retreat in January 2019, I alerted ministerial colleagues that 'the retreat provides the opportunity for ministers to have first-hand information and knowledge about the performance management contract that they will be signing with the President'.[14]

In general, there are two tiers of the public sector performance management system in the governance of the country, operating at institutional and individual performance management levels. In the context of the New Direction administration, the innovative framework included Tier 1:

---

[13] See Annex 3 for a List of the GoSL Ministries between 2018 – 2023, First Term administration of President Bio

[14] Chief Minister's Statement , Second Cabinet Retreat, 10-11 January 2019.

1. Ministerial Performance Management and Performance Management of Legislative Agencies within the Office of the President: led by the Chief Minister and the Office of the Chief Minister (OCM)
2. Departments, Agencies, Commissions, State-owned Enterprises, Parastatals, Tertiary Institutions, and Local Councils – led by the Ministry of Planning and Economic Development (MoPED).

Tier 2 included:

1. Individual Performance Contracts for Officers in Grade 11 and above – led by Cabinet Secretariat (CabSec)
2. Individual Performance Appraisals for Officers in Grade 10 and below – led by Human Resource Management Office (HRMO)

To deliver an effective ministerial performance management framework, the Office of the Chief Minister implemented a lean and efficient performance management structure that included:

1. Directorate of Service Delivery and Performance Management led by a Director General, as the Technical/Professional arm of the Office of the Chief Minister, and was headed by an experienced international civil servant, Mr Edward Kamara.
2. Director for Policy, Planning, and Strategy
3. Director for the Free Quality Education (FQE): Monitoring and Evaluation, on a 50-50% job-share between the Office of the Chief Minister and the Ministry of Basic and Senior Secondary Education
4. Director for Health, Monitoring, and Evaluation with a 50-50% job-share with the Ministry of Health and Sanitation.
5. Director - Office of the Chief Minister – MoPED Coordination on Monitoring and Evaluation, on a 30% job-share with OCM
6. Director for Performance Management Follow Up with the Cabinet Secretariat on a 20% job share with OCM.

It was agreed that since MoPED had the ministerial statutory responsibility for planning, monitoring, and evaluation, it would take direct responsibility for the performance management of all SOEs, parastatals, and local councils. To facilitate the implementation of an effective performance management process across government, a joint coordinating, monitoring, and evaluation framework was developed between MoPED and OCM and led to the creation of the National Monitoring and Evaluation Directorate (NAMED).[15]

The Ministerial Performance Management methodology covered the following targets: i. Strategic Leadership; ii. Fiduciary Management; iii. Strategic Planning; iv. Corruption Eradication. The Quarterly Ministerial Performance Management process ensured that each ministry was graded based on these four performance targets and ranked as 'Excellent Performance', 'Performing Ministry', or 'Underperforming, needing additional leadership support'.

With the support of DSTI, the Office of the Chief Minister established a 'One-Stop-Shop' governance E-Dashboard for the monitoring of the Ministerial Performance Management and the achievement of targets for the Manifesto, the Human Capital Development priority, and the Medium-Term National Development Plan. This governance E-Dashboard portal was only accessible to the President, vice president and chief minister. The rationale was that the president and vice president could at any moment and in real time, review and monitor the performance of ministers as a governance accountability and transparency tool.

On 7th February 2019, President Bio signed the first Ministerial Performance Contract with each Cabinet Minister as a monitoring tool to account for governance service delivery and the performance of ministers in achieving the New Direction government agenda. At the official signing of the Ministerial Performance Contract at State House, President Bio stated that:

> The aim is to hold the Ministers and their Deputies accountable to the people of Sierra Leone. . . . The Ministerial Performance Management will ensure and strengthen effective public service delivery that would positively impact on the lives of the people. . . .By signing the Ministerial Performance Management Contract, a culture of service delivery responsiveness will be established and maintained across government. . . .This contract will improve government's effectiveness in service delivery, develop a culture of accountability and trust in the public

[15] This led to the creation and legislation of the National Monitoring and Evaluation Agency (NaMEA) by an Act of Parliament in 2024 in the Office of the President to provide technical leadership, monitoring and coordination of the national monitoring and evaluation agenda.

> sector, transform the negative image of public servants and political leaders through performance and service delivery, create value for money and clear understanding of incentives and sanctions for service delivery. . . .I want us to deliver tangible results that will have impact on the lives of Sierra Leoneans. Most Sierra Leoneans have lost trust in government but as a new government, we are changing that narrative now and I need you all to show leadership in your respective Ministries.[16]

To be clear, ministerial performance management and contracts were not new and had been a feature of the 11-year APC administration of President Koroma, supported by the Tony Blair Africa Governance Initiative. As Chief Minister, I was also aware of the negative media coverage of the ministerial performance contract during the administration of President Ernest Koroma, claiming that the performance management of ministers failed to achieve meaningful results or impact on the lives of Sierra Leoneans. Critics argued that the ministerial performance contract was a mere façade; in their view, it failed because the administration prioritised political loyalty over accountability, retaining ministers despite evidence of incompetence or corruption.[17]

The *Sierra Leone Telegraph* Newspaper editorial, in commenting on the signing of the Ministerial Performance Contract by President Bio, raised the pertinent governance question, stating that 'The key question is when underperforming ministers and those found to be corrupt under this leadership — that have been appointed to office because of their role in helping the President win the 2018 elections — will be sacked and not simply transferred into key positions in Cabinet reshuffles. People voted for change in March 2018. They are now looking to President Bio to deliver that change'.[18]

---

[16] State House Press Secretary, 'Statement by His Excellency President Julius Maada Bio on the Official Signing of the Ministerial Performance Management Contract' 7th February 2019.

[17] Sierra Leone Telegraph, Abdul Rashid Thomas, 'President Bio has signed Ministerial Performance Contract –now up to Ministers to deliver' 8th February 2019, www.thesierraleonetelegraph.com)

[18] Ibid.

Ministerial Presentations to the President: What Happened to Underperforming Ministers?

To support the effective implementation of the Ministerial Performance Management and to create a positive environment of collective ownership of the process, I organised another framework of ministerial presentations to the president. The primary objective was to provide the president and presidency (i.e., vice president, secretary to the president and presidential advisers) the opportunity to have understanding and appreciation of the work, mandate, and programmatic responsibilities of each of the ministries, as well as the opportunity for the President and the Presidency to critically review, in person and on the spot, the work of the ministry in service delivery of the administration's agenda.

The Ministerial Presentation to the President involved the outline of what each ministry was required to do, and the presentation at State House was led by the minister, the permanent secretary and professional heads of the ministries. The ministerial presentation to the president was one of the most popular governance tools but was equally loathed by some colleague ministers. Those high-performing ministers and ministries often relished the moment of formal presentation of the work of their ministries to the presidency. For them, it was a moment to 'shine' and secure the confidence of the President, demonstrating that they were up to the task that the President appointed them to do, thereby ensuring their survival in the post during any Cabinet reshuffle. On the other hand, those ministers and underperforming ministries typically showed strong aversion to any such ministerial presentation to the presidency, and often sarcastically commented, without any justification, that the 'chief minister is trying to get them sacked from their roles'.

The Ministerial Presentation to the President was a very good governance delivery tool because I observed, firsthand, how the President, Vice President, Secretary to the President and Presidential Advisers would master the Ministerial Presentation Briefs submitted in advance and the constructive comments to support the leadership capacity development and service delivery of the Ministry. The Permanent Secretaries and Professional Heads of the ministries were often the most impressed because, for the majority of them, that was the only opportunity to meet with the President and be in the same conference room with the Presidency. The only challenge for this initiative was the difficulty of scheduling this item into the president's crowded schedule.

To further strengthen the enhancement of service delivery performance management culture and to create incentives for ministerial performance, the Office of the Chief Minister organised the first-ever *Best Ministerial Performance Management Award,* presented by President Bio to the three high-performing ministries in December 2020, and they included:

i. Ministry for Finance for the competent financial management and making sure that essential commodities were available in the country during the COVID-19 pandemic
ii. Ministry of Defence and Ministry of Health, a joint award for the effective management of the COVID-19 pandemic in the country.
iii. Ministry of Basic Education for the effective service delivery relating to the implementation of the Free Quality Education.

What happened to underperforming ministers and the efficacy of monitoring performance management? During my tenure, those ministries that consistently failed the Ministerial Performance Management Review, with a ranking and scorecard of less than 30% in all four target areas, were referred to the president for review and advice. I am aware of an instance where the president directed the secretary to the president to write strongly worded warning letters to five underperforming ministers. Four of the underperforming ministers were later replaced in a Cabinet reshuffle, but one of the underperforming ministers was reassigned to a lesser role as State Minister. In fact, two of the ministers sacked deliberately failed to even sign the ministerial Performance Contract with the president.

Clearly, the concept and practice of ministerial performance did not go down well with colleague ministers and, to put it most charitably, was hated and detested by some colleague ministers simply because they are not used to being performance managed, monitored, and reviewed. For those close to the President as allies and friends, it was assumed that they did not need to be performance managed, nor did they need to show to the President that their ministry was performing well. For them, their close relationship with the president was the 'letter of credit' and guarantee for the retention of their jobs whether they are performing or not! As such, some ministerial colleagues 'recruited' their permanent secretaries to undermine the ministerial performance management review and submission process, often unfairly criticising and taking out their frustrations on the OCM Directorate for Service Delivery Performance Management.

Governance Coordination and Follow-Up Role of Chief Minister: Inter-Ministerial Committee on Sectoral Issues

Governing a country and running the affairs of a state is one of the most difficult, complex, and challenging tasks. It is not only a thankless job because of the unending criticisms, but also it primarily involves putting together programmes, projects, some with quick-impact or medium- to long-term impact, and planning and implementing complex systems, policies, structures, processes, and rules that are used to direct and manage the affairs of the state. It involves creating decision-making authorities, defining how decisions are made, oversight and monitoring performance, and ensuring transparency and accountability amongst the diverse stakeholders. Governing a country also involves managing the oversight of other branches of government, such as the legislature and judiciary as well as conducting the external relations of the country. In effect, governing a country is like an elephant; you can hardly see all the parts of the animal at the same time.

It is made worse by the fact that colleague ministers, presidential appointees, heads of SOEs, parastatals and commissions, parliamentarians from the same ruling party often deliberately undertook actions to undermine and delay the implementation of programmes/projects and even presidential directives as long as it did not serve their vested 'resource-extraction' and neo-patrimonial accumulation interests. As such, skillful management and efficient political and economic management of state affairs were paramount and a key to this is coordination and follow-up to enhance service delivery.

Coordination is one of the important roles of the Chief Minister that was not often publicly acknowledged, because of its rather mundane technical process. There are a lot of major governance sectoral issues that cannot be realistically delivered by one government agency or ministry, and as such, they require inter-agency or inter-ministerial coordination.

The concept and practice of Inter-Ministerial Committees emerged from governance meetings chaired by the President or Vice President and at Cabinet meetings that required the input, collaboration, sharing of expertise and competences of other ministries and agencies of government to enable the delivery of a particular sectoral and cross-cutting issue. Therefore, as chief minister, my role was to facilitate these inter-ministerial sessions and brief the President on the outcomes. This reporting structure was vital for securing the necessary executive backing and clarifying the next steps for governance delivery. A key component of the function of the Inter-Ministerial Committee was site and field visits to the affected areas, communities, and projects to ensure that the deliberations and recommendations of the Committee were based on facts and evidence on the ground.

To this end, I convened and chaired several such Inter-Ministerial Committees, including

1. Inter-Ministerial and International Partners Group Committee on Education/FQE
2. Inter-Ministerial Committee on Lands and Water Catchment Areas
3. Inter-Ministerial Committee on National Examination Malpractices
4. Post-Mudslide Disaster and Humanitarian Response Inter-Ministerial Committee
5. COVID-19 Preparedness Stakeholders Inter-Ministerial Committee
6. Agriculture Strategic Plan (Rice Value-Chain Production) Inter-Ministerial Committee
7. School Bus Commissioning and Distribution Inter-Ministerial Ad Hoc Committee
8. GoSL ICT / Digitisation Policy Inter-Ministerial Committee
9. Roads for Development Inter-Ministerial Committee
10. Inter-Ministerial/Sectoral Committee to Support Office of the First Lady's 'Hands Off Our Girls' Programme
11. E-Government Infrastructure Inter-Ministerial Committee.

Inter-Ministerial/Sectoral Committee to Support Office of the First Lady's 'Hands Off Our Girls' Programme: Impact and Controversies

The Inter-Ministerial/Sectoral Committees were not just to conduct and follow up on key governance cross-cutting issues, but importantly, they served as a platform to solve or resolve critical governance matters that required the direct intervention or decision-making input of the President.

The implementation of the Office of the First Lady's 'Hands Off Our Girls' program serves as a prime example of the governance hurdles inherent in high-profile initiatives. It surfaced significant conflicts over policy ownership and the integration of specialised programs into the broader governmental framework. The GoSL constituted Ministries mandated with responsibilities for the welfare of children and children's affairs in the country raised the legitimate concern that the Office of the First Lady's 'Hands Off Our Girls' programme was a conflict of interest and amounted to a usurpation of the constitutional and mandated responsibilities of the Ministry of Social Welfare and the Ministry of Gender and Children's Affairs. Understandably, the two GoSL Ministries did not take kindly to the First Lady's 'Hands Off Our Girls' advocacy and intervention programme for children's affairs across the country. Both ministries perceived this as an unconstitutional and unnecessary shift of power, resources, and official functions from the mandated GoSL ministries to the Office of the First Lady.

To resolve this governance challenge, in view of the potential added value and complementarity of the advocacy interventions of the First Lady's 'Hands Off Our Girls' programme, President Bio directed the Chief Minister to convene a high-level stakeholders meeting at State House. To this end, a high-level, inter-ministerial, and cross-sectoral meeting was convened on 19th September 2019, chaired by the President. The high-level meeting was attended by the First Lady, Madam Fatima Bio; the Finance Minister, Hon. Jacob Jusu Saffa, the Minister of Social Welfare and Children's Affairs, Hon Baindu Dassama; the Secretary to the President, Dr. Julius Sandy; and the Chief Minister.

The important outcomes of this high-level meeting included:

1. That the Office of the First Lady's 'Hands Off Our Girls' Programme be considered as a GoSL Development Project to

complement the GoSL Human Capital Development Programme and the GoSL Medium-Term National Development Plan.
2. That the GoSL support for the First Lady's 'Hands Off Our Girls' programme should be intra-governmental and multi-sectoral, with core seed funding from GoSL to leverage international development funding and donor technical support.
3. The Ministry of Finance recommended that, for budgetary allocation purposes from the GoSL Consolidated Revenue Fund, the Office of the First Lady's 'Hands Off Our Girls' programme be considered a GoSL Development Project with a designated budget line appropriate for the Office of the First Lady and separate from the GoSL budget line for the Office of the Secretary to the President.
4. The imperative to 'projectise' the Office of the First Lady's 'Hands Off Our Girls' programme by developing it as a bankable development project for international donor support.
5. The evident need to strengthen capacity building and development of the Staff in the Office of the First Lady through specialised 'secondment' placements from the GoSL HRMO and technical assistance support from donors.
6. The Office of the First Lady to submit a fully costed short-, medium-, and long-term strategic plan of activities and to submit for the allocation of seed funding from the Ministry of Finance
7. To're-direct' some donor-funded projects to NGOs relating to children and children's affairs in the country, to be channeled for implementation through the Office of the First Lady.
8. That the Ministry of Social Welfare and Children's Affairs lead on the development of an early child marriage policy change.
9. That the Chief Minister convene regular quarterly cross-ministerial and sectoral meetings to resolve the conflict of mandate, roles, and responsibilities, as well as to identify cross-cutting priorities in support of the welfare of children.

Evidently, the outcome of this high-level meeting was laudable because it brought together all national-level stakeholders to focus on developing programmes, interventions, and strategic policies for the development and advancement of the welfare of children in Sierra Leone. This high-level meeting recognised the important advocacy role and interventions of the Office of the First Lady and the imperative for all sectors and ministries to work collaboratively to promote and deliver services for children, in particular, the girl child.

To this end and as Chief Minister, I joined the First Lady to attend several high-level meetings with development partners to solicit donor funding and technical assistance to support the Office of the First Lady's 'Hands Off Our Girls' programme.[19]

Notwithstanding, and despite my vast experience and expertise in peacemaking, conflict mediation, and resolution, I failed to resolve the fundamental and legitimate concerns raised by the Ministry of Social Welfare and the Ministry of Gender and Children's Affairs as to who or which institution or agency had the principal mandate and constitutional role in the GoSL to lead on issues pertinent to children and children's affairs in the country. In fact, the recommended follow-up inter-ministerial/sectoral meetings were never held because of fundamental differences in the governance approach and personality differences in the running and management of state affairs.

Clearly, the high-level advocacy interventions of the First Lady's 'Hands Off Our Girls' programme across the country and internationally directly led to the creation of a new dedicated GoSL Ministry of Gender and Children's Affairs; the parliamentary legislation and enactment of a new Child Rights Act 2024 as well as the new Prohibition of Child Marriage Act 2024.

However, the executive decision to make the Office of the First Lady's 'Hands Off Our Girls' programme a GoSL 'Development Project', funded from the Consolidated Revenue Fund, was in hindsight, a 'political power decision'. A 'political power decision' is simply when the constituted political authority makes decisions and governance choices that influence government policies, institutions, outcomes, and procedures within a specific context or for a specific purpose. In this specific context, the 'political power decision' on 19th September 2019 made by the executive leadership inevitably ended up negatively impacting the powers, authority, role, and mandate of the constituted GoSL Ministry of Social Welfare and the Ministry of Gender and Children Affairs that have the constitutional and legislative mandate for all matters pertinent to children and the welfare of children in Sierra

---

[19] One such high-level meeting took place in November 2019, where the First Lady and I, met with the wife of the former British Prime Minister, Mrs Cherry Blair, in Abu Dhabi, United Arab Emirate.

Leone. Simply put, this well-intentioned executive-level 'political power decision' invariably undermined the relevance and efficacy of the constituted GoSL ministries appointed by and created by the President.

CHAPTER FOUR

Strategic Policy & Building State Governing Institutions: National Disaster Management Agency and Independent Commission for Peace and National Cohesion

Introduction

An important role of the Chief Minister was to lead on national strategic policy formulation and implementation on behalf of the Presidency or as assigned or delegated by the Executive President. This strategic policy role of the Chief Minister led to the formulation of the following: the National Disaster Management Agency; the Independent Commission for Peace and National Cohesion; Sierra Leone National Reforestation and Timber Governance Policy for the establishment of National Reforestation and Timber Governance Agency in collaboration with the Ministry of Agriculture & Food Security and Ministry of Environment & Forestry; Policy for the Cultivation of Cannabis Sativa for Medical and Industrial Use, in collaboration with the Ministry of Health and Sanitation; and the proposed National Plastic Management Policy.

This chapter examines how, why and when, as Chief Minister, I led the establishment of the following state governing institutions such as the National Disaster Management Agency (NDMA) as a permanent structure for disaster preparedness and resilience; Bintiumani III for national dialogue for peace and national cohesion, and the Independent Commission of Peace and National Cohesion (ICPNC) as a permanent infrastructure for peace in post-war Sierra Leone. The chapter also critically explores the politics of institution building and how the recurrent and entrenched nature of domestic politics undermines and detract from the professional, technocratic and 'interest-free' process of governance institution building for the benefit of the people of the country.

National Disaster Management Agency: Permanent Institution for Disaster Preparedness and Resilience

The establishment of a permanent national disaster management body has been a long-standing governance imperative. Since independence in 1961, the absence of a dedicated and responsive institutional framework has left the country vulnerable, making the creation of such an authority a critical priority for national resilience. The country has faced periodic disasters, both man-made and nature-induced, creating persistent and unnecessary deaths of thousands across the country, especially in the topographically challenged and hilly capital city, Freetown, with its notoriously poor drainage system and sanitation. Apart from the perennial flooding, on 14th August 2017, Freetown was devastated by a large-scale mudslide after a heavy and persistent downpour of rain, causing the death of more than 1,000 people and the devastation of property.

The new administration of President Bio inherited the public fallout and lack of access to humanitarian relief supplies for some of the victims of the Mortomeh/Sugarloaf mountain mudslide in August 2017. As chief minister, I was directed by President Bio to lead on the facilitation of humanitarian relief supplies to the mudslide victims. I constituted an ad hoc Inter-Ministerial Committee comprising the Ministry of Lands, the Ministry of Social Welfare, and the Ministry of Tourism to lead on and coordinate the distribution of the relief supplies to the Mortomeh mudslide victims and government cash payments to victims who had been directed to relocate or lost their properties during the mudslide disaster.

During the commemoration of the first anniversary of the Mortomeh mudslide disaster at St. Paul's Catholic Church, President Bio expressed the urgent need to have a dedicated national agency for disaster management and preparedness. Faced with the recurrent calamities of the man-made and nature-induced disasters, the president directed that, as chief minister, I lead on the development of a national policy and agency for disaster preparedness, management, and response.

In pursuance of this Presidential Directive and in collaboration with the Office of National Security (ONS), hitherto responsible for all national disaster management and response matters in the country, a national disaster management policy was developed by ONS. I presented the National Disaster Management Policy paper to Cabinet, which was adopted, and Cabinet specifically mandated the establishment of a National Disaster Management Agency, authorising the Chief Minister to collaborate with the Attorney General and Minister of Justice and ONS in the creation of a new National Disaster Management Agency to be legislated by Parliament and supervised by the Office of the President. Effective collaboration between the Office of the Chief Minister, ONS, and the Office of the Attorney General and Minister of Justice led to the parliamentary ratification and legislation of the first-ever National Disaster Management Agency Act 2020.

The NDMA Act provided for the 'establishment of a National Disaster Management Agency to manage disasters and similar emergencies throughout Sierra Leone, to establish national, regional, district, and chiefdom management committees, to establish a National Disaster Management Fund to provide finances for the prevention and management of disasters and similar emergencies throughout Sierra Leone...'[1]

Section 3 of the Act states that 'The Governing Body of the Agency shall be the National Platform for Disaster Risk Reduction, which shall be responsible for the control and supervision of the agency'. Section 3, 2(a) stipulated that the 'vice president shall be the chairman' of the National Platform, and Section 28, 1, vests the President with the power and authority to convene and declare a State of Disaster Emergency, stating, 'The President may declare a State of Emergency in accordance with Section 29 of the Constitution of Sierra Leone, 1991 (Act No. 6 of 1991) where the National Platform establishes the imminence or prevalence of a disaster to the president'.[2]

On 19th November 2020, Sierra Leone's first-ever National Disaster Management Agency was officially launched by President Bio at State House. In commending the governance institution-building effort, President Bio stated,

> We made a commitment in the New Direction Manifesto to "remove disaster management from ONS and establish a specialized national agency for disaster preparedness and management". . . .So our establishment of the National Disaster Management Agency was a

[1] The National Disaster Management Agency Act 2020, signed 8th June 2020 by H.E. Dr. Julius Maada Bio, President of the Republic of Sierra Leone, p. 2

[2] Ibid, 2020.

> promise made. Today, it is a promise delivered. . . .Beyond a promise kept, the National Disaster Management Agency is a permanent institution for making our country more resilient. . . .Let me publically thank the Chief Minister for his leadership in making this Agency possible.[3]

In my statement as Chair of the official launch event, I reassured that 'The ONS has an existing Directorate for Disaster Management, so the new National Disaster Management Agency will hit the ground running because the ONS will provide the institutional home for the core expertise to help the operationalisation of the Agency. Second, we have indication of committed and enthusiastic bilateral and multilateral donors who are on standby to support the operationalization of the Agency'.[4]

The inaugural Director-General, Lt. Gen. (Rtd) Brima Bureh Sesay, assured that: ' The Agency will strive towards accomplishing various targets and indicators encapsulated in the Sendai Framework agreed by the UN Disaster Risk Reduction, ensure implementation of the African Risk Reduction, and work towards effective enforcement of the National Disaster Management Agency Act 2020'.[5] International partners such as the World Bank country manager, Gayle Martin, confirmed the bank's support for the multi-disciplinary and cross-cutting work that the new NDMA will embark on, stating, 'managing disaster risk requires a high-level of coordination and convening power to work across a variety of stakeholders and sectors. The NDMA, therefore, requires the authority and ability to activate, or cause to activate, national emergency measures at the time of a disaster. It is also required to convene MDAs across sectors at the highest level –both during times of emergency as well as in disaster prevention and preparedness'.[6]

---

[3] Statement by H.E. President Julius Maada Bio on 19th November 2020 at the Official Launch of the NDMA at State House.

[4] Chief Minister, Professor David Francis' Statement at the Official Launch of the NDMA at State House on 19th November 2020.

[5] Statement by DG – NDMA, Lt. Gen. Brima Bureh Sesay, on 19th November 2020.

[6] Statement by World Bank Country Manager, G. Martin, Sierra Leone Telegraph, 28th November 2020, 'World bank Support Sierra Leone's Disaster Emergency Preparedness and Response Plan'. www.sierraleonetelepgrahp

Politics of Parliamentary Ratification of the NDMA Act 2020

Inevitably, Sierra Leone's complex governance landscape—shaped by deeply entrenched domestic politics and vested interests —ensured that even this technocratic institution, designed solely for the public good, was not immune to the corrosive effects of the 'politics of decline.' The institutional intent was benign, yet its implementation was immediately caught in the crossfire of historical entrenched interests and partisan friction. From my technocratic governance perspective and, in particular, because the President had given the instruction and mandate to establish this new National Disaster Management Agency, I never expected anyone to even try to undermine the process or go against the directive of the President. I was simply wrong!

During the parliamentary debate on the ratification of the NDMA Bill, I was covertly informed that there were 'malignant elements' within our own New Direction administration who wanted to 'hijack' the powers and authority of the new disaster agency. The contentious issue and controversy revolved around who should be designated in the NDMA Act as the person with the 'power and authority' to declare a disaster emergency and the power and authority to convene high-level MDAs and international actors to activate and cause the implementation of disaster emergency measures at the time of a disaster. Desperate and covert efforts were made to 'insert' into the final version of the NDMA Bill a provision that granted the 'Chairman of the National Disaster Risk Platform', as stipulated in Section 3, 2 (a), the 'power and authority' to declare a disaster emergency when a disaster happens and with the convening 'power and authority' for a disaster emergency.

To put it most charitably, I was shocked by such a brazen attempt at usurpation of power and authority because the primary responsibility and constitutional power to declare any disaster emergency is the sole mandate and responsibility of the president. This is the governance practice across the world. Globally, only the president or prime minister or head of state has the constitutional power and executive authority to declare a disaster emergency because the president/prime minister/head of state, has to make real-time, life or death decisions relating to the evacuation of all or part of the population from the disaster-stricken area or the threatened area to 'temporary shelters for the preservation of life' or the power to authorise the deployment and mobilisation of the military and security forces as well as the release of public and private personnel to render disaster emergency service.

Why the attempt to subvert the globally established standard and governance practice in disaster emergency in the creation of our own national disaster management agency? Based on my extensive informal and covert consultations with trusted SLPP, APC, C4C, and NGC[7] parliamentarians, I was reliably informed that the 'fight' about the NDMA Bill was simply about who will control the prospective national and international resources when the NDMA is established and operationalised. With the impasse in Parliament on the draft NDMA Bill, I took my legitimate concerns to President Bio, whose intervention led to the resolution of the attempt to 'capture' the new disaster management agency for private and neo-patrimonial benefits and resource accumulation. The 'compromise' led to the final version of the NDMA Bill and Act authoritatively stipulating Section 28, granting the President the sole power and authority to declare a disaster emergency.

It may well have been that without my assertive and uncompromising technocratic governance intervention, the country might well have ended with a national disaster management agency and Act without the president and head of state as the one with the sole power and authority to declare disaster emergence in the country. To illustrate why this is important, the Wellington Fuel Tanker disaster on 5th November 2021 that claimed the lives of 150 people was the first major disaster and test case to verify the effective disaster emergency response and intervention of the newly created NDMA and the implementation of its disaster response structures. This fuel tanker disaster happened whilst President Bio was out of the country and the Vice President was Acting President and Chairman of the National Platform for Disaster Risk Reduction. Despite the physical absence of the President from the territory of Sierra Leone, the Chairman of the National Platform, the then Acting President and substantive Vice President, Dr. Juldeh Jalloh, and the NDMA governing body had to refer all matters to the President, as per Section 28 of the NDMA Act 2020, for all critical matters and decisions relating to the need or

---

[7] The National Grand Coalition (NGC), a breakaway faction from the SLPP, and the Coalition for Change (C4C), a splinter group from the APC, were minor political parties in Parliament between 2018 – 2023.

otherwise for a declaration of a disaster emergency in the Wellington disaster-stricken area.

Bintumani III[8]: National Dialogue for Peace and National Cohesion

Between 2014 and 2017, I had extensive intellectual and practical governance discussions with President Bio, then studying at the University of Bradford's Department of Peace Studies for his doctoral degree, about the need for post-war Sierra Leone to build a permanent infrastructure for peace. In fact, I had just published a new book *When War Ends: Building Peace in Divided Communities* (2012)[9], in which I argued that there is no development without peace and that peace, security, and stability are necessary prerequisites for long-term development and socio-political progress in any country. On the assumption of the mantle of state governance, President Bio directed that I put into practice my academic and policy-practice knowledge on how to build peace and reconcile the bitterly divided communities in Sierra Leone.

As Chief Minister, I was aware of the fact that the divisive political tensions and landscape in the aftermath of the 2018 general and presidential elections that sent the APC into political opposition after 11 years of ruling the country, was not conducive to the peace, security, stability, and development of the country, in particular, keeping the new government on track and able to focus on service delivery for the people. Based on this appreciation of the 'Peace-Development Nexus' in post-war and transition societies like Sierra Leone, I advised President Bio to convene a Bintumani III national consultative conference on peace and national cohesion with the specific objective to build a permanent infrastructure for peace in the form of an Independent Commission for Peace. President Bio, in his State Opening of Parliament address on 10th May 2018, called for the establishment of an

---

8 Bintumani I national consultative conference was convened on 14 – 17 August 1995 under the National Provisional Ruling Council (NPRC) military regime to agree on the restoration of a peace timeframe for end of war and the return to civilian democratic rule. Bintumani II was convened on 7-9th April 1999 to consult on the pathway to peace and the end of the civil war.

9 David J. Francis, 'When War Ends: Building Peace in Divided Communities' Aldershot, Ashgate, 2012.

Independent Commission for Peace and National Cohesion, stating, 'Mr Speaker, to promote unity and national cohesion, my government will launch a presidential initiative that will be heralded by a national conference on peacebuilding, diversity management, and the rebuilding of national cohesion. I therefore announce the creation of an Independent Commission for Peace and National Cohesion to be established by an Act of Parliament'.[10]

With this presidential directive, as chief minister and in collaboration with the Ministry of Political and Public Affairs, I organised and co-chaired the Bintumani III National Consultative Conference on 23 – 24 May 2019 at the Bintumani International Conference Centre. It was one of the most anticipated and highly attended national consultative conferences in post-war Sierra Leone. It brought together a broad range of national stakeholders, including all political parties, civil society organisations, inter-religious groups, students representatives, women's groups, diplomatic and development partners, and international resource persons from the UK, Rwanda, Ethiopia, and Kenya.

At the Bintumani III national consultative conference, President Bio was emphatic in his statement on 23 May 2019 that:

> We are gathered here Today to take a major step in strengthening our democracy and consolidating peace through a consultative conference that will lead to the establishment of an Independent Commission for Peace and National Cohesion. . . . Both Bintumani I and II were consultative conferences. . . . convened to present the view and expectations of the people and to make informed decisions about the shared direction and destiny of our nation. . . .The Bintumani III conference is about soliciting the views of Sierra Leoneans on the remit, the shape and the mechanics of the proposed Independent Commission for Peace and National Cohesion. The eventual establishment of that Commission will be a huge step in efforts to further consolidate and strengthen our democracy and peace. . . . 28 years after the adoption of our national constitution, 18 years after the end of the civil war, 15 years after the conclusion of the Truth and Reconciliation hearing, through 5 democratic elections cycles and 3 peaceful transfers of power, I want to encourage all of us to continue

[10] State House Press Secretary, 'State Opening of Parliament Address on 18th May 2018 by H.E. President Julius Maada Bio.

> our efforts to build solid institutions that will enable us to consolidate democratic practices and enhance peace and national cohesion.[11]

Bintumani III was a paradigm shift in consolidating post-war peacebuilding, and this directly led to the establishment of the Independent Commission for Peace and National Cohesion. The Bintumani III national consultative conference was therefore a deliberate agenda-setting process to shape the post-war peacebuilding environment in the country by focusing the national attention on dialogue on how, as a nation, we build a national infrastructure for peace, owned by the people and more akin to the process of 'people building and winning' peace in war-torn and post-conflict societies.[12]

In my statement as co-chair, I made an impassioned plea that the Bintumani III national consultative conference was about the 'future of our children', stating that 'Sierra Leone today is at a crossroad because half of the people in the country are desperately trying to lift and push the country up the hill of progress, development, peace, and stability. But the other half of the country, without realising it, is trying to pull the country down the hill and keep the country where it is: poor, underdeveloped, divided, and full of political tensions. But this is not and must not be the future of this great and beautiful country – the only place that we call home!'.[13]

As expected, the call for a national conference on peace sparked manufactured friction along party lines. Bintumani III was subjected to a campaign of deliberate misinformation that sought to undermine its credibility and distort the public's understanding of its transformative goals. In fact, the main APC opposition party officially refused to participate in a national dialogue conference on peace and national cohesion, but some high-profile senior APC politicians attended the conference, stating that it was in the national interest to have done so.

The controversies and media hype, in particular, the politically motivated misrepresentation of the proposed Bintumani III, forced me

---

[11] State House Press Secretary, 'Keynote Address by H.E. Dr Julius Maada Bio, President of Sierra Leone at the National Consultative Conference at the Bintumani International Conference Centre on 23 May 2019.

[12] David Francis, 'When War Ends', 2012.

[13] State House Press Secretary, 'Statement by Chief Minister, Professor David Francis, at the Bintumani III National Consultative Conference on 23 May 2019 at Bintumani International Conference Centre.

to categorically state what the national consultative conference was not about and its primary objectives, arguing:

> Bintumani III is not about the on-going Commissions of Inquiry because Bintumani III had no mandate to end the Commissions of Inquiry legislated by Parliament, Not about Corruption Allegation Cases, Not about the current Elections Petitions in Courts because the Government will not interfere in the judicial process and the Rule of Law. . . .Bintumani III is not a Truth and Reconciliation platform and that Sierra Leoneans should not expect former Ministers or Government Officers turning up to say sorry for any corruption allegations and asking for forgiveness. The purpose of Bintumani III is to bring everyone together in an inclusive process to discuss how to build an infrastructure for peace in the form of an Independent Commission for Peace and National Cohesion as announced by President Bio. . . . Bintumani is simply about establishing the foundation for inclusive peace in the New Sierra Leone that the TRC Report called for and to lay the long-term and resilient foundation for non-violent conflict resolution…[14]

Independent Commission for Peace and National Cohesion: Building Infrastructure for Peace

With the presidential announcement in Parliament in May 2018 on the establishment of an Independent Commission for Peace and National Cohesion as well as the successful outcome of the Bintumani III National Consultative Conference, the Office of the Chief Minister secured the support of UNDP to fund the commissioning of a Green Paper to look at the mandate, rationale, and governance structure of a national Peace Commission.[15] The revised strategic policy paper and

---

[14] Ibid, 23 May 2019. The Sierra Leone Truth and Reconciliation Commission (TRC) was created as part of the Lome Peace Agreement to end the 11-year brutal civil war in July 1999. The TRC Report of 2004 and the TRC Act of 2000 made four main recommendations on how to build a new Sierra Leone based on democracy, rule of law, end of corruption and sustainable peace.

[15] The Office of the Chief Minister recruited two (1 local Sierra Leonean and 1 International) peacebuilding and national governance experts to draft the Peace Commission policy paper. State House Press Release on the UNDP funded Green Paper provided 'Update on the Establishment of an Independent Commission for Peace and National Cohesion, 22th November 2018. Madam Hawa Samai, later

Cabinet White Paper on the establishment of an Independent Commission for Peace and National Cohesion were approved by Cabinet and authorised the Chief Minister to collaborate with the Attorney General and Ministry of Justice to progress the parliamentary legislation of the Independent Commission for Peace and National Cohesion. The Peace Commission was legislated by Parliament on 20th December 2020, after a high-political drama in the Wells of Parliament.

The Independent Commission for Peace and National Cohesion Act, 2021 (Act 3 of 2021), 'confers on the Commission the power to take measures to prevent, manage, and resolve conflicts; to build, promote, and maintain sustainable peace in Sierra Leone. . .'[16] The Act invested the ICPNC with 17 key functions and powers, including:

1. 'To undertake measures to prevent, manage, and resolve conflicts, to build, promote, and maintain sustainable peace in Sierra Leone and to advise the Government of Sierra Leone, on all aspects of conflict resolution and peace'.[17]
2. 'promote peace, reconciliation, and unity in Sierra Leone' (Section 12, 2 (a);
3. 'build peace cultures, enhance tolerance, and support peaceful resolution of conflicts throughout Sierra Leone' (Section 12, 2 (b);
4. 'monitor and evaluate the implementation of the Truth and Reconciliation Commission recommendations. . .' (Section 12, 2 (c);
5. 'advise the government on the formulation and implementation of policies relating to peacebuilding, conflict prevention, and conflict resolution' (Section 12, 2 (d);
6. 'develop programmes and provide services that promote awareness activities in local communities, schools, and local

appointed as the First Executive Secretary of ICPNC, was the local consultant and Professor Owen Greene at the Department of Peace Studies, University of Bradford, served as the International consultation for the Green Paper. Dr Lansana Gberie, the current GoSL Ambassador to Geneva / Switzerland, supported the review and editorial work of the Green Paper.

[16] Independent Commission for Peace and National Cohesion Act, 2021, Published in Sierra Leone Gazette 5 on 4 February 2021.

[17] Section 12, 1, of the ICPNC Act 2021

administration to promote conflict prevention and conflict resolution' (Section 12, 2 (e).[18]

Importantly, the Act granted independence to the Commission in Section 13: 'In the discharge of its functions under this Act, the Commission shall not be subject to the direction or control of any person or authority'. The Act also vested in the Commission the powers of the 'High Court', stipulating in Section 12 (3), 'For the purposes of an investigation under this Act, the Commission shall have such powers, rights, and privileges as are vested in the High Court in a trial…'[19]

To operationalise the ICPNC Secretariat, the ICPNC was officially launched on 20th April 2023 at the Bintumani International Conference Centre[20]. President Bio had earlier appointed the governing board of the Commission on 13 July 2021.

High Political Drama and APC Opposition Party Walk-Out in Parliament on Peace Commission Bill

As always with the context of governance in Sierra Leone, the creation of the Peace Commission was not spared from the entrenched nature of domestic politics and political party divide. In the week leading to my appearance in Parliament in December 2020 to present the ICPNC Bill for parliamentary debate and ratification, I was confidentially informed that the main APC opposition was determined to derail the legislative process of ratifying the Peace Commission Bill.[21] With that prior confidential alert, I came prepared with substantive and authoritative knowledge to defend the Peace Commission in Parliament. I was also reassured that our ruling SLPP Parliamentarians as well as leading MPs in NGC, C4C, and even the main opposition APC, would support the parliamentary ratification of the Peace Commission Bill and the enactment of the ICPNC Act because it was in the national interest.

---

[18] Ibid.

[19] Ibid.

[20] Noticeably, the President and Vice President were absent at the formal launch of the ICPNC. The official launch, on behalf of the President, was by the then Chief Minister, Mr. Jacob JusuSaffa who served in the role from 2021 – 2023.

[21] As Chief Minister, I built a quiet, trusted and confidential relationship with all the influential leaders of the political parties including the SLPP, APC, NGC and C4C.

The political divide reached a crescendo when the APC parliamentary membership walked out of the well of Parliament during the enactment of the ICPNC Bill, signalling their rejection of the consultative process. The public walkout of the main APC opposition in Parliament on a national peace initiative was captured LIVE on national TV, which provoked a negative public and media reaction against the APC opposition party.

From an opposition party politics standpoint the parliamentary walk out was a high-profile political tactic and stunt by the APC opposition to show their displeasure against President Bio's New Direction administration. Additionally, the walk-out was specifically designed to publicly embarrass the Chief Minister and former Governance Transition Team Chairman, who had used 'colourful' and 'divisive' language to describe the 11-year rule of the APC as 'egregious corruption' and 'organised criminal racketeering enterprise'. For this rather unfortunate description, I understand, a directive was issued by the Party hierarchy to walk out on the Chief Minister in Parliament as a protest against the allegation of politically targeting the APC opposition. Who would have rationally imagined that Members of Parliament would walk out on a national interest and public good matter like the ratification and legislation of a permanent infrastructure for peace so that 'Never Again' Sierra Leone would suffer the scourge of war and violence? This is what the negative nature of domestic politics, based on self-interest, sectional and particularist-interests does in the governance of state affairs.

Failure of Some Strategic Policy and Governance Institution Building Interventions

The establishment of the NDMA and the ICPNC followed the effective governance tradition of SLPP governments in leading on the building of state governing institutions, such as the President Ahmad Tejan Kabbah-led government between 1996 and 2007, in establishing post-war state governing institutions such as the Anti-Corruption Commission (ACC), the National Revenue Authority (NRA), and the National Social Security and Insurance Trust (NASSIT). The spectacular achievement in building governance institutions should not mask the reality of the failure of some strategic policy and institution-building interventions.

As Chief Minister, and despite all the political influence and governance leverage that I had access to, it was not possible to push Cabinet approval for the following strategic interventions, though Presidential approval had been granted, and they include: the National Reforestation and Timber Governance Policy for the establishment of the National Timber Governance Agency in collaboration with the Ministry of Agriculture and Food Security and the Ministry of Environment and Forestry; the Policy for the Cultivation of Cannabis Sativa for Medical and Industrial Use, in collaboration with the Ministry of Health and Sanitation; and the National Plastic Management Policy. By all indications, these are critical governance issues that affect the lives of the citizens, so why the failure to secure approval, or why were these strategic policies 'quietly shelved'?

The strategic policy on reforestation and timber governance agency was designed as the first-ever, national-level approach to effectively and sustainably manage the country's forest and timber resources with the establishment of a legislated Timber Governance Agency. Historically, timber had been one of the most lucrative forestry exports for Sierra Leone, yet it remained largely and deliberately unregulated. In fact, according to the Ministry of Finance domestic revenue mobilisation data, timber export sales between 2018 and 2019 made a 3-4 percent contribution to the GDP annually.[22]

The primary concern was that the unregulated exploitation of our forest resources had caused massive degradation of the environment, endangering the flora and fauna, and potentially setting in place future environmental disasters. Compounding the situation, the unregulated harvesting and transportation of timber logs by heavy-duty vehicles across the country had devastating impact and destruction of newly constructed feeder roads and bridges, especially during the rainy season between May and September. Due to the negative impact of this problem on the local road networks, President Bio directed the Security Sector, including the Ministry of Defence and the Ministry of Internal Affairs, to impose a seasonal ban on the transportation of timber during the rainy season. The Office of the Chief Minister was instructed by the President to monitor the implementation of the seasonal ban on the transportation of timber across the country. In announcing the annual

[22] Ministry of Finance Data on Domestic Revenue Mobilisation 2020.

suspension of timber logging and transportation of logs, the GoSL press release stated, 'All logging and transportation of timber products are suspended for five months'.[23]

The serious concern about the negative impact of the unregulated exploitation of the country's timber resources and the potential environmental impact led to the international ban on the export of timber from Sierra Leone by the Convention on International Trade in Endangered Species (CITES) in 2021. The following were banned from Sierra Leone under the CITES international environmental laws, including Afzelia Africana (locally known as 'Lenge), Pterocarpus Erinaceus (Gbenni), and Erythrophleum Suaveolens (African Rosewood). The export permits for these species were rejected due to concerns about the sustainability and legality of the trade. The CITES concern was legitimate in that the international trade data on the import of rosewood to China showed a phenomenal increase in exports from Sierra Leone since 2018. Imports from Sierra Leone into China were highest in 2018 at 225,560 mt, which, according to CITES, reached 'levels more than three times higher than the previous year and accounted for over half of imports from Sierra Leone, as high as 80%....Sierra Leone has become the largest exporter of rosewood in recent years'.[24]

It was this serious national concern about the unregulated exploitation of the country's forestry resources and negative environmental impact that prompted the Office of the Chief Minister to commission a policy paper on national reforestation and the creation of a Timber Governance Agency as a service delivery strategy to address this problem.[25]

Again, the embedded, if not virulent, interest-based nature of governance and domestic politics immediately kicked in because such a

---

[23] Government of Sierra Leone Suspends Timber Logging and Transportation, 31st May 2022

[24] CITES _ Sierra Leone: Compliance Status, August 2021; CITES, Biennial Report for Sierra Leone CITES Management Authority for the Period 2020 – 2021; CITES, National Report, IUCN, 2020.

[25] Dr Abu Bakar Massaquio & Mr Baimba Abdulai Koroma, 'National Reforestation and Timber Governance Policy: Policy for the Establishment of a National Reforestation and Timber Governance Agency (NARTGA), Office of the Chief Minister, GoSL, December 2019.

national timber governance framework was perceived as not in the best interest (private accumulation) of the GoSL Sole Timber Agent and the then Ministry of Agriculture and Forestry. The Office of the Chief Minister was discouraged from progressing the proposed National Reforestation and Timber Governance Agency policy paper to Cabinet, and it was quietly shelved.[26]

However, a positive outcome was that, in collaboration with the newly created Ministry of the Environment (MoE), the Office of the Chief Minister supported the planting of 1.2 million trees across the country as part of the New Direction government's National Tree Planting and Reforestation programme, funded by the GoSL Sole Timber Agent through the Ministry of Finance. In addition, though we failed to create a national timber governance agency to regulate the timber trade and the exploitation of the country's forest resources, a new amended Forestry Act 2022 was legislated to replace the outdated Forestry Act of 1988.[27]

Similarly, the strategic policy papers and high-level consultations with the respective ministries and government agencies relating to addressing the national menace and health hazard of plastic pollution, as well as the economic and health benefits from a policy on Canabis sativa for medicine and industrial use, did not progress and were put on the backburner because they were perceived as not politically expedient to progress such politically sensitive policy.[28]

The case of plastic pollution and the negative environmental impact was instructive. Across the country, plastic pollution was and is a major environmental challenge, with massive waste, in particular, single-use plastics, contaminated land, beaches and waterways. Urban plastic

---

[26] Draft Cabinet Paper, Memorandum by the Chief Minister, Sierra Leone National Reforestation and Timber Governance Policy 2020, January 2020

[27] GoSL, The Forestry (Amendment Act) Act 2022,

[28] Medical Cannabis Sativa refers to the controlled cultivation and scientific industrial production for medical purposes and medicinal use. It has emerged as a multi-billion pharmaceutical industry business, especially in Western countries and more recently in some African countries. The nine Africa countries that have legalized medical cannabis sativa include: Malawi; Zambia; South Africa; Zimbabwe; Lesotho; Ghana; Morocco; Rwanda and Uganda. See: Antonio A. T. Junior et al, Unlocking the Socio-economic Advantages of Cannabis Sativa & Legalization in Africa Countries: an in-depth review, Global Journal of Agricultural Research, Vol. 11, (1), 2023, pp. 32 – 52.

pollution is characterised by a high volume of street-dumped waste, particularly sachets, which make up 70 per cent of the 80 per cent of plastic discarded in cities like Freetown. Inadequate waste management infrastructure and low recycling of plastic waste are part of the severity of the plastic pollution, with significant environmental, public health and economic impact on the ecosystem.

Given the severity of the problem, the President indicated the policy intention to ban single-use plastic, as in the case of other Africa countries that have banned single-use plastic such as Rwanda, Kenya, Tanzania, South Africa, Uganda, Ethiopia, Botswana, Nigeria, Morocco, Mali and Cameroon.[29]

Despite the best efforts of the Office of the Chief Minister to mobilise national support from the Ministry of the Environment and the private sector plastic industries, nothing came out of this effort. In fact, powerful and entrenched interest groups in the Plastic Industry sector coalesced to prevent any further action taken within the mandate of the MoE.

To all intents and purposes, these national-level policy failures that would have had significant impact on improving the lives of the people and enhancing service delivery, demonstrated the simple fact that the entrenched and rent-seeking nature of neo-patrimonial governance accounts for why and how Sierra Leone is permanently described as poor and underdeveloped.

---

[29] 34 Plastic Bans in Africa: A Reality Check, GreenePeace Africa, 19 May 2020

CHAPTER FIVE

Chief Minister Special Emissary Missions and International Engagements Roles

Introduction

In addition to the diverse high-profile roles and mandate of the Chief Minister, there were numerous additional functions that the Chief Minister was required to perform or undertake by virtue of being one of the Principal Advisers to the President.[1] These additional roles included the official requirement to be part of the President's high-level delegation and Presidential entourage at local and national events; official Presidential functions and the protocol requirement to sit at the High Table with the President; Special Emissary/Special Envoy Representative missions on behalf of the President at local and international levels; and being part of the Presidential delegation attending international events.

Let me put these diverse and numerous roles of the chief minister in context, and with the benefit of hindsight and first-hand experience of closely working with President Bio, I now know that the role of President and the enormous weight and burden of running a country is one of the most difficult and challenging tasks. The fact of the matter is that the citizens expect the President to have ALL the ANSWERS to their problems and the many challenges faced by the country. They also routinely BLAME the president or hold him accountable for ALL the PROBLEMS faced by the country, especially when it comes to the existential necessities and livelihood of food, shelter, health, employment, and transportation, i.e., the so-called 'bread and butter' or 'rice and cassava leaf sauce' aspects of daily life.

With this enormous burden and weight of expectation, the president therefore assigns duties and delegates responsibilities to the vice president, the chief minister, and appointed ministers and public officers

[1] The President is authorised by Sections 40, 53 and 56 of the 1991 Constitution to assign duties and delegate responsibilities.

as a strategy of sharing the huge load of governing a country or statecraft burden-sharing.

Presidential Special Emissary/Special Envoy Role

To illustrate this presidential burden of sharing responsibility, as chief minister, I was often directed by the president, often at short notice, to intervene in the mediation and resolution of a local crisis situation that had the potential to threaten the peace, security, and stability of the country. Other such special emissary roles may just be fact-finding missions to help inform the President or the Presidency in reaching rational and evidence-based strategic policy decisions or governance intervention for service delivery, such as the recurrent Sa-Malen Chiefdom palm oil plantation workers' dispute with the Socfin Agricultural Company in Pujehun district, Southern Sierra Leone.

To this end, when the Sierra Rutile Mine Workers Union went on strike in November 2018, withholding their cooperation with the Australian-based Iluka Resources principal investor[2], I was directed by President Bio to lead the mediation and resolution of the Mine Workers strike action by visiting the Sierra Rutile mining site in Sembehun/Mokanji.[3] The Sierra Rutile Mine Union Workers' strike action had a potential negative economic and financial impact on the inherited struggling economy. As such, the new administration could not countenance the disruption of mining operations and the much-needed mineral revenue.

The Sierra Rutile strike was of such magnitude and threat to the profitable operations of the mining company that it required the visit of the Iluka Resources Managing Director and Chief Executive Officer (CEO), Tom O'Leary, to Sierra Leone. The mine workers strike mediation team visit to the Sembenhun/Mokanji site was preceded by a high-level meeting between President Bio and the Iluka Resources CEO and its leadership team in Sierra Leone. The high-level mediation intervention led to the resolution of the mine workers' dispute with Iluka

---

[2] Sierra Rutile was a subsidiary of the Iluka Resources, operating and mining rutile and sands assets in Sierra Leone for over 50 years. Rutile export is a major revenue generator for GoSL.

[3] The Mediation Team included the Minister of Mines & Mineral Resources; the Minister of Internal Affairs; the Minister of Information & Communication and the State House Press Secretary & Presidential Spokesman.

Resources and the resumption of mining operations on 4th December 2018. The Sierra Rutile–Iluka Resources press release on the resolution of the mine workers strike stated, 'His Excellency the President has intervened to assist in the resolution of the dispute. This has followed further strike action taken by the workforce. Following the meeting on 26th November 2018 between the company's subsidiary, Sierra Rutile Limited (SRL), the United Mineworkers Union, and the Government of Sierra Leone, including the vice president, the chief minister and other senior ministers, the president has established a task force in support of resolving the issues between the union and SRL.[4]

By all indications, this type of governance intervention by the Chief Minister, as directed by the President, justified the governance wisdom of the President to create the position of the Chief Minister in the process to directly support the President in sharing the burden of state governance responsibilities and to deliver services to the people. Resolution of the Sierra Rutile strike action was a direct governance service delivery intervention for the Morkanji mine workers and the protection of their jobs and the livelihoods of their families.

International Engagements as Part of Presidential Delegation and Special Envoy Role of Chief Minister

The international engagement and special envoy roles of the Chief Minister are not only about being part of the president's high-level delegation and representation at these external events, but also, importantly, about participating in these high-level deliberations as well as following up on important actionable decisions and projects to be implemented.

In pursuit of this assigned responsibility, and to this end, between 2018 and 2021, as Chief Minister, I accompanied and was part of the President's high-level delegations for state visits to strengthen bilateral relations and external engagements with the following countries: Qatar, Turkey, the United Kingdom, Senegal, Cote d'Ivoire, The Gambia, Guinea, Mali, Ghana, the UEA, and Nigeria.

In addition, I was a regular member of the president's high-level delegation to participate in high-level international and multilateral

[4] Sierra Leone Telegraph, 'Sierra Rutile Mining Operations Resumes as Workers Agree to Return to Work', 4 December 2018.

events such as the United Nations General Assembly (UNGA) in 2018 and 2019; the state visit to China and participation at the Forum for China – Africa Cooperation (FOCAC) in September 2018; the Tokyo International Conference on African Development (TICAD) in Tokyo in 2019; the UK- Africa Investment Summit in London in January 2020; and the ECOWAS Summit in 2019.

Perhaps, the most notable, if not, infamous, external participation as part of the President's delegation was President Bio high-level visit to the European Commission in February 2019. Though the visit itself was very successful because the GoSL was able to secure a total grant of €245 million, the rather embarrassing protocol drama at the office of the European Commission President did not go unnoticed and was hugely frowned upon by President Bio.

To be clear, the GoSL delegation did not create this embarrassing diplomatic and protocol blunder. It turned out that on the day of the high-level visit, the EU Ambassador to Sierra Leone, Tom Vens, who was part of the high-level meeting in Brussels in the Office of the European Commission President, Jean-Claude Jaunker, had inadvertently given a very 'exaggerated' briefing introduction of who the Chief Minister, Professor David Francis, was in the GoSL. It was open diplomatic knowledge that the European Commission President, Jean-Claude Juncker, was widely known for his rather unpredictable and erratic, often undiplomatic behaviour. On this fateful day, I was at the back of the delegation when we arrived at the Office of the Commission President. I was horrified to hear the Commission President shouting my name in front of President Bio, 'Where is the Chief? Where is the Chief?'. On meeting Commission President Juncker, he greeted me effusively as if we were 'old-time friends or buddies', to the amazement of President Bio and the rest of the delegation, but much to my mortified embarrassment. Clearly, such undeserved praise and welcome of the Chief Minister, right in front of President Bio, was not only a serious breach of diplomatic protocol but also equally a completely disastrous disrespect to the President and a breach of the very first law of the *48 Laws of Power*, which warned, 'Never Outshine the Master'.[5]

Notwithstanding, as Chief Minister, I led a high-level GoSL delegation to Moscow, Russia, to participate in a 3-day investment conference in June 2019 at the invitation of the Russian Federation

---

[5]Rober Greene, '48 Laws of Power', 1998.

Ministry of Industry and Trade on the theme 'Harnessing Emerging Partnership in an Era of Rising Protectionism'. The investment conference was organised under the auspices of President Vladimir Putin and jointly by Afrexim Bank. During the conference, I used the platform to 'market' Sierra Leone as an attractive destination with significant investment opportunities to establish new economic partnerships and cooperation with emerging markets. The participation of the GoSL delegation was part of President Bio's efforts to attract external investment to finance the construction of the USD $1.8 billion Lungi Bridge project, linking Freetown and the country's international airport.

CHAPTER SIX

Conclusion: Lessons in Statecraft

Politics of the Role of Chief Minister: Achievements, Problems, and Challenges

The position of the Chief Minister and my appointment to the role by the New Direction Government of President Bio were within the constitutional mandate and prerogative of the president to support the executive presidency in the administration of the affairs of the State and governance service delivery. President Bio assigned and delegated diverse functions and responsibilities to the chief minister, always providing the necessary presidential support, authority, and power to ensure that the chief minister competently and professionally delivered on all the roles and mandates of the Office of Chief Minister. Even those who may have disliked the creation of the post of Chief Minister as an innovative governance structure, as well as those who did not like the postholder, all agreed that as chief minister, I brought gravitas, respectability, decorum, professionalism, disciplined leadership and competence in managing the affairs of the state. This professionalised and technocratic governance approach was perceived by the citizens as a welcome break from the previous nepotistic, privatised, rent-seeking, and 'PadiPadi' (informal and friendship-based) governance status quo. One interlocutor from the main APC opposition party, in commending the professionalised and disciplined approach to state governance-stated: 'When dɛn Say Chief Minister Professor Francis de kam, everybody no say nar Soba Bisnɛsɛn nor to PikinPle' (When they announce the arrival of Chief Minister Professor Francis, everyone knows that this is a serious matter and not child's play').[105]

This book has documented in detail, providing facts and evidence to illustrate that it was strategic leadership on the part of President Bio to appoint the position of Chief Minister and, in the process, supported

105 Confidential discussion at a Public Event with a senior APC leader and former Vice President of the Sierra Leone.

the effective governance of the state in modern Sierra Leone. The diverse roles and numerous responsibilities assigned or delegated by the president led to spectacular achievements, which bolstered the confidence of the citizens in the New Direction Government. These achievements included serving as one of the principal advisers to the president and how this directly led to the promulgation of the Presidential Executive Order No. 1, which, among other things, re-introduced Sunday commercial and trading activities banned during the Ebola epidemic in 2014 and introduced a national cleaning day on the first Saturday of each month.

Serving as de facto presidential speechwriter directly influenced the presidential declaration of three 'peacetime democratic wars' on i. corruption, ii. indiscipline, and iii. poverty as well as influenced the announcement of 20% domestic revenue contribution to GDP as the basis for future government financing of Independence/National Day Celebrations.

The governance service delivery achievements led to the organisation of cabinet/ministerial Retrcats to develop a high-performing ministerial team to deliver the government agenda and the prioritisation of the Manifesto commitments, as well as political and administrative interface high-level retreats for civil servants, parliamentarians, SOEs, commissions and parastatals. Importantly, a major achievement was the rolling out, management, and implementation of the Ministerial Performance Management to ensure service delivery of results impacting on the lives of the people. In addition, the strategic policy and governance institution-building role of the chief minister led to the establishment and legislation of the first-ever National Disaster Management Agency (NDMA) and the Independent Commission for Peace and National Cohesion (ICPNC). In collaboration with the MoEF, we led the National Tree Planting programme by planting 1.2 million trees across the country. In collaboration with the Ministry of Technical and Higher Education, I visibly supported the establishment of three new public universities and the parliamentary enactment of the 2021 Universities Act that created the Eastern Technical University, Kono University for Science and Technology, and the Milton Margai Technical University. Furthermore, in collaboration with the Cabinet Secretariat and DSTI, with the strong support of the Vice President, I led the introduction of the Virtual

Cabinet Meetings during the COVID-19 pandemic as part of the E-Government infrastructure capacity building.

In all the determined efforts to make governance work in Sierra Leone and for the New Direction Government to succeed, as Chief Minister, I was intellectually, practically, and ideologically (i.e., Social Democratic values) convinced that there is a moral purpose behind the delivery of targets and results/outcomes and that purpose is to achieve the common good for all, i.e., the desire and effort to change the lives of the people for the better, such as providing access to affordable electricity and clean drinking water for all or making sure that children go to school and acquire quality education for free or affordably for the poorest of the poor. Holding the Office of the Chief Minister was not just another job but a passionate mission to create a ladder of opportunity for all to achieve their dreams and aspirations as well as to contribute to the common good that benefits all Sierra Leoneans irrespective of the regions, social status, ethnicity, religion, and political party.

Notwithstanding, there were equally spectacular failures that gave harsh lessons in governance. The diverse and numerous roles and responsibilities carried out by the Chief Minister inadvertently created the tendency to overshadow the President and Vice President, thereby generating unnecessary media controversies and distractions from the primary focus of the efficient political and economic management of the State and results-based governance delivery to change the lives of the people who voted for Change and New Direction. With the benefit of hindsight, the Chief Minister's role should not be the media news item and focus, but rather the President and Vice President.

In fact, taking on too many responsibilities assigned by or delegated by the President was simply a recipe for failure. In delivering on the roles and functions assigned as Chief Minister, I took an unrealistically ambitious governance approach, believing that everyone will and must support the president's agenda, thereby leading to the failure to create a Presidential Executive Office to make the Presidency efficient; the failure to secure Cabinet approval to establish the first-ever National Reforestation and Timber Governance Agency; as well as the failure to deliver on the menace and health hazards of plastic pollution, even with the support of the MoEF.

In implementing the Ministerial Performance Management and Contract, I should have 'worn a more politically savvy hat' in working with colleague Ministers by appreciating their genuine sensitivities and concerns about the ministerial performance contracts. This quasi-political-technocratic posture would have drastically reduced the recurrent accusation by some colleague ministers that I was 'difficult to work with and too strict'.

With these diverse responsibilities, following up on key governance delivery initiatives and projects persistently posed a major challenge, and as such, as chief minister, I was not able to follow up with the leadership of the public Higher Education sector/universities to develop and submit a strategic policy document and roadmap on the future of education in Sierra Leone, against the background of the successful introduction of the Free Quality School Education. Importantly, as chief minister, and understandably, I failed to successfully provide leadership to implement some of the key governance reform recommendations in the GTT Report as authorised by Cabinet on 6th July 2018, beyond the establishment of the Judge-led Commissions of Inquiry and Commissions of Inquiry (CoI) Report and findings.

Chief Minister as a Governance Delivery Development Actor

The important governance roles and functions performed by the Chief Minister and the proximity to the President as the centre of political and economic power invariably put the Chief Minister in a powerful and influential position to do a lot of good for the people and serve as a de facto 'development actor'. Between 2018 and 2021, I found myself in the opportune situation of initiating, promoting and supporting the implementation of key development projects of lasting impact on the lives of the people. Two notable examples are i. my leadership in securing the funding and construction of the Sengbe Pieh Memorial Bridge at Juba/Lumley in Freetown and ii. Kenema City development projects.

Sengbe Pieh Memorial Bridge in Freetown

It is important to note that 99 percent of the Sierra Leone population do not know that I initiated and secured the major funding for the construction of the Sengbe Pieh Memorial Bridge. How did this happen? During a courtesy call by the Chinese Ambassador Hu Zhangliang, in November 2018, as Chief Minister, I raised the difficult problem of the Juba Wallace Johnson Bridge and how the inordinate traffic delays were not only bad for vehicular traffic but also for the economic and commercial well-being of the western part of the city of Freetown.[106] I requested support from Ambassador Hu Zhangliang for the Government of China to finance the construction of a new second bridge at Juba/Lumley to ease the traffic menace. I justified the request to Ambassador Hu that it was a quick-impact project and a visible demonstration that the Government of China supported the new Bio administration. This was an audacious request on my part because I shrewdly capitalised on the unconfirmed allegations raised in the media in the run-up to the March 2018 general and presidential elections that the Government of China supported the APC Ernest Koroma government.[107]

Ambassador Hu agreed to secure Government of China funding for the construction of the new second Juba/Lumley bridge on the condition that the GoSL should cover one-third of the funding and that the bridge will be constructed within six months by a Chinese company. I took this initiative, and the confirmation of the Chinese Ambassador to President Bio, who graciously approved the second Juba/Lumley bridge project and instructed the Minister of Finance, Jacob Jusu Saffa, to allocate the requested counterpart one-third funding.

The 1.8 metre bridge, built in five months and jointly financed at USD $1.9 million, was officially commissioned by President Bio on 25 April 2019 as the Sengbe Pieh Memorial Bridge, linking the Lumley and

[106] I leave at Goderich, western Freetown, and had firsthand daily experience of the major traffic bottleneck created by a single bridge with 2 vehicular lanes.

[107] I have examined this unfounded allegation in my book, 'China – Sierra Leone Relations: Friendship, Cooperation and Win-Win Diplomacy, 2024.

Juba communities in the west end of Freetown.[108] On the part of GoSL, the Chairman of the Presidential Infrastructural Initiative (OPII), Dr. John Tambi, worked with the Chinese Embassy construction company to secure the speedy construction of the bridge. During the commissioning ceremony, Ambassador Hu Zhangliang acknowledged the astute leadership that I brought to securing the joint financing of the bridge project as well as the professionalism that I demonstrated in the implementation of the bridge construction project.

Kenema Development Interventions

Anyone familiar with the mainstream SLPP politics knows that the Kenema District is the heartland of the SLPP support base in the eastern region.[109] To be clear, I am a 'son of the soil' of Kenema,[110] so the people of Kenema and the district were very happy and grateful to President Bio for my appointment as Chief Minister, the first senior Cabinet appointment from the district and region in decades.

However, there was a major problem in Kenema. Kenema District and the Eastern region, including Kailahun and Kono, had been largely neglected during the 11-year rule of the APC administration in terms of development project interventions. By 2017, Kenema City was an eyesore, with pothole-ridden main streets in the centre of the city. Internal discord also plagued Kenema, which was essentially a 'divided

[108] It was President Bio's unique idea to name the second Juba /Lumley bridge as the Sengbe Pieh Memorial Bridge as a way of honouring the nation's heros. Historically, Sengbe Pieh was a Sierra Leonean Slave in America (1813 – -79), then known as Joseph Cinque in USA and became famous for his role in the Amistad Revolt, an historical event that was fictionalized in the blockbuster Hollywood movie, *Amistad Revolt.*

[109]Kenema District has 11 Members of Parliament and 16 Chiefdoms. Kenema is historically infamous and during difficult internal SLPP political contestations, has served as a 'swing' region, siding with the opposition political party, APC, leading to the SLPP loss of political power as in 1967 and 2007. Kenema is historically credited for siding with the then Flagbearer aspirant, Julius Maada Bio, originally from the South, and overwhelmingly supported his bid to successfully win the contest as the SLPP Presidential Candidate in 2017.

[110] I was born in Kenema, did my primary (St Paul's) and secondary school (Holy Trinity) education in Kenema and all my deceased family members are buried in Kenema.

family'. The presence of various acrimonious factions created a volatile environment for implementing the administration's local development agenda.

It was in this volatile and divided political environment that I emerged as a development actor by virtue of my senior government role as Chief Minister from Kenema. After careful consideration and political guidance from President Bio on how to positively engage with Kenema, I was mandated to lead on the reconciliation and development of Kenema as an urgent local political priority. To this end and with the strong and consistent support of President Bio, the following development projects were successfully implemented:

1. Built Unity, Reconciliation, and Peace for Kenema Development. The first challenge was how to achieve peace and unity in a divided Kenema. Using all my peacemaking, conflict resolution, and peacebuilding skills, I used an inclusive and collective ownership approach to ensure that everyone owned the development and socio-economic progress of Kenema. With the authority and gravitas of the status of Chief Minister and with the widespread knowledge of the support of President Bio for the development of Kenema, everyone came onboard to progress the development projects, which I branded the 'New Kenema for Peace, Unity, and Development'. Nevertheless, peacebuilding is rarely about the total elimination of friction. Although the factions in Kenema remained, the process succeeded in channeling their energy toward a shared goal. For the first time, these diverse groups moved past their acrimony to support a unified roadmap for Kenema's development. I recall at the monthly Kenema Stakeholders meeting that I convened, the SLPP Chairman, Dr Prince Harding, was invited to one of such meetings to support the local reconciliation and peacebuilding process. Dr Harding characteristically and wittingly commented that 'Only Chief Minister Professor Francis can bring together cats and dogs to sit at the same high table for Kenema deliberations'. Though the audience found his blunt comments humorous, it was a tacit confirmation of the efforts made to win the peace and bring the previously divided city together to achieve the common goal of developing Kenema.

2. 21 Tarmac roads constructed by First Tricon and Pavi Fort construction companies, including completion of the main city centre streets such as Blama and Hanga roads, Dama Road, Koroma Street, Circular Road, Massaquio Street, Ngobulando Street, etc.
3. New Kenema iconic and modern Clock Tower funded by Africell, with the support of the First Lady, Madam Fatima Bio
4. New Kayfrey Bridge replaced the colonial bridge at the entrance of Kenema city
5. Supported the Mayor of Kenema to complete the construction of the new Kenema City Hall, a project started in the 1980s
6. New Kenema Town Football Artificial Turf, donated by SLFA with FIFA funding
7. Donated a 32-seater air-conditioned bus to the District Football team in the Premier League –Kambio Eagles
8. Led the establishment of the new Eastern Technical University to replace the Kenema Polytechnic and the establishment of an Endowment Fund for the new university.
9. Financially supported the major refurbishment of the Kenema Central Mosque and St Paul's Cathedral.
10. With President Bio's support, sponsored 15 pilgrims from Kenema District for Hajj in Mecca
11. Established the Eco Rice Production Company as a mechanised rice cultivation and production enterprise to support food security in the district and created more than 150 jobs for people in the Small Bo/Blama and Nongowa Chiefdoms.
12. With support from the Roads Maintenance Fund (RMFA) and to prevent large-scale flooding, and in collaboration with the Mayor of Kenema and Town Chief of Largo Jasawabu[111], led the construction of culverts and drainages in Kenema Waman-Abu Road area and Largo Village.
13. With the support of the Minister of Energy, Alhaji Kanja Sesay, secured the construction of an electricity sub-station in Largo Village that ensured the electrification of Largo Jasawabu and its environs.

[111] Largo Jasawabu is my maternal village and the home village of the Paramount Chief of Nongowa Chiefdom, Kenema District. PC Sadique Kapuwa Mateo III.

14. Financed the purchase of a local health centre premises for the Kakajama community, benefiting access to healthcare delivery, including maternity service, for more than 2,000 people.

Technocratic Governance Leadership vs. Nature of Domestic Politics and Political Culture

As one of the key principal advisers to the President, I saw my role as Chief Minister as the main tool to protect the reputation of the President and the New Direction government as well as to prevent, where possible, any scandal that would have potentially damaged or discredited the Presidency and the government. Hindsight has made it clear that I initially underestimated the power of entrenched interests and the domestic politics to influence the Chief Minister's mandate. I have to accept that my early approach did not sufficiently account for the weight and impact of a political culture that often resists standardised governance and reform. It is surprising that as far back as 2016, i.e., two years before my appointment as Chief Minister and joining the government as a senior Cabinet Minister, I had forcefully argued in one of by books in which I criticised the subversion of the Social Contract in Sierra Leone my the small predatory and self-serving ruling and governing elites in the country, irrespective of the political party divide, stating that:

> As such, politics, and more precisely holding public office, irrespective of political affiliation and ideological persuasion (often, the majority of the political elites do not even have or believe any politico-development ideology), is simply about the rule and dominance of the rather small ruling and governing political and economic elites who have become guarantors and gatekeepers of this neo-patrimonial state based on extractive and predatory social contract. For the kleptocratic elites, their first basic instinct (prebendal) when elected or appointed to any public office is to steal and amass wealth. Wealth, political power, socio-economic and development opportunities and privileges are only opened to and re-cycled amongst the small political elites, thereby increasing elite wealth and power as well as perpetuating the grip of the political elites in Sierra Leone. It really does not matter which political party is in power, either APC or SLPP, the story is the same. In effect, the

> extractive and predatory social contract in Sierra Leone partly explains the persistent poverty, underdevelopment and violent competition amongst the ruling and governing elites for access and control over state power as manifested by successive military coups and the civil war. Post-war Sierra Leone is a divided society along wealth, power, access and entitlement to basic services and existential necessities of life (food, shelter, education, healthcare and employment). The majority of the population and, in particular, the rural poor, are permanently red-lined into poverty and deprivation, with generations entrapped into a vicious cycle of poverty trap. The political elites have incentive to maintain the extractive and predatory social contracts because the status quo benefits them.[112]

As Chief Minister, after 25 years of residing in England as a high-profile senior African academic and policy adviser to a number of Western and African governments and multilateral institutions, I was unprepared for the harsh realities and challenging context of the nature of domestic politics and negative political culture whereby governance is extremely 'informalised' to the point that the state governing institutions are subverted to serve the interest of the 'self' and the ruling and governing elites in power before any form of professional and disciplined achievement of service delivery results and outcomes for the people. It took me a full year to appreciate and understand the extent of how the 'Shadow State'[113] practically operated, the key actors and players, and the 'soft underbelly' of politics and governance in contemporary Sierra Leone.

The point that I am making, in terms of lessons in statecraft, is that while there is huge value in appointing someone who has been out of the country for a number of years and as such insulated from the pervasive and corrosive rent-seeking networks of the nature of domestic politics, the lack of knowledge and appreciation of how the 'Shadow State' operates in practical terms in Sierra Leone significantly impacted my performance and service delivery role as chief minister. With the

---

[112] David J. Francis et al (eds.) Peace, Democracy & Development in Africa, Adonis & Abbey, London, 2016, pp. 87 – 88.

[113] William Reno, 'Corruption and State Politics in Sierra Leone' Cambridge University Press, 1998; 'Warlord Politics and African States', Lynne Rienner, Boulder, 1999; Jean Francois Bayart, 'The State in Africa: the Politics of the Belly' Polity Press, 1993.

benefit of hindsight, and as the GTT Chairman, I would never have used such colourful and divisive language as 'egregious corruption' and 'organised criminal racketeering enterprise' in the GTT Report of July 2018.

Evidently, the public highly appreciated my role as Chief Minister in the effort to professionalise the running of state affairs based on competence, disciplined, as well as strong and assertive leadership to primarily focus on making sure that the delivery of the New Direction administration's agenda was the number one priority. Working across government, with colleague ministers, permanent secretaries and civil servants, the GoSL agencies, departments, SOEs, commissions, and the private sector economic, commercial, and financial operators and their leadership, all demonstrated in our many and diverse engagements and governance interactions, that they valued and appreciated my chief minister's technocratic governance leadership and often perceived this as a breath of fresh air from the 'government business as usual status quo'.

Managing the Chief Minister and the Hubris of 'Outshining the Master'

Without overemphasing the point, the post of the chief minister is a very powerful and influential role in the governance structure of modern Sierra Leone, as a unitary state, with a republican constitution and a presidential system of government. In *Governing a Poor Country* and serving as Chief Minister, I have presented a candid and critical reflection as well as an in-depth outline of the roles, functions, and achievements as well as the controversies, problems, and challenges associated with the post of Chief Minister and its governance delivery methodology.

The numerous and high-profile roles and functions that I performed as Chief Minister did provoke legitimate concerns, especially among the political elites, but at the same time, there was widespread support and admiration for the new kind of professional, disciplined, and competent leadership that was not motivated by the negative dimensions of the nature of domestic politics and 'Shadow State' political culture. In fact, Dr. Abdulia Conteh forcefully lamented that:

> In view of the numerous roles and significant powers and functions officially assigned to the Chief Minister, the public perception is that it would appear President Bio is leading but he is not in charge. The Chief Minister vested with such significant powers seems to suggest that the President has removed some functions from his office to that of the office of the Chief Minister thereby reducing the role of the Presidency. It is not surprising to hear many citizens say that the leader they voted for has less influence in the day-to-day running of the Government than the Chief Minister. Many also tend to believe that while the President is the 'Face of the Country' he the, President, wields a lot less power and the government is actually being controlled by a more influential figure in the person of the Chief Minister who holds much practical power in the everyday affairs of the Government.[114]

With this rather constructive but politically motivated view from Dr Conteh, who had vast and demonstrable experience in the governance of Sierra Leone, as chief minister, and with the benefit of hindsight, I may have forgotten the practical leadership advice of Robert Greene when he aptly admonished in the 'First Law of Power' in his *48 Laws of Power* book that 'Never Outshine the Master. . . . Always make those above you feel comfortably superior'.[115]

Nevertheless, in the performance of my diverse functions as Chief Minister, I never deliberately acted or actively sought the media limelight or tried to 'outshine' the Principal, in this case, President Bio. As a political scientist, I knew that the worst mistake for any public figure, minister, or politician is to do anything or try to act in ways that will 'outshine the principal or master'. Driven by both professional ethics and a personal history of trust, I prioritised the President's public profile and image above all else. I worked tirelessly to ensure he was perceived as a leader of global stature, focusing the narrative on his statesmanship and his role as the primary architect of the New Direction. At all official events, I always introduced him as 'His Excellency Brig Gen (Rtd) Dr Julius Maada Bio….'. At official functions, both nationally and internationally, I was always at his side, as protocol demanded, but always two steps behind him. I seldom gave media interviews as chief

[114]SierraEye, March – May 2020, p.11.

[115] Robert Greene, '48 Laws of Power' Profile Books, 1998, p. ix.

minister to promote myself, because I clearly understood that it was not the business and role of the chief minister to go on media self-publicity or give media interviews because I knew that the State House Press Secretary, the Presidential Spokesman, the Minister of Information and Communication, and the respective Ministers were the main actors and best suited to communicate what the government was doing, rather than the Chief Minister.

However, my concerted efforts not to 'outshine the Principal/Master', i.e., President Bio, in hindsight, my assertive, competent, disciplined, and determinedly professional service delivery activities and interventions might have inadvertently and unknowingly created what Robert Greene warned against: '. . . do not go too far in displaying your talents or you accomplish the opposite – inspire fear and insecurity'.[116]

With this critical context, the governance structure of the role and mandate of the Chief Minister meant that the chief minister was not only supervised and managed but also importantly subordinated to the President and Vice President as per Sections 40, 53, 54, and 56 of the 1991 Constitution. On several occasions the President instructed Vice President Juldeh Jalloh to supervise and monitor the service delivery interventions of the chief minister, which created a good professional working relationship with the Vice President.

Therefore, those who claim that the role of the Chief Minister usurped the constitutional function and mandate of the Vice President are simply wrong. The constitutional role and mandate of the vice president as the 'principal assistant' to the president are stipulated in Section 54. At no time did my role and functions as Chief Minister usurp, duplicate, or clash with the constitutional mandate of the Vice President. If anything, there was never any clash between the vice president and I, in the performance of our separate roles and functions. The Vice President and I had a very cordial and mutually respectful professional working and personal relationship. In fact, the vice president would go out of his way to defend my role as chief minister and often reminded me that 'competence gets you the job, but politics keeps you in the job'.

116 Robert Greene, 48 Laws of Power, 1998.

This is not to say that our working relationship was always perfect because there were instances of clashes of views on fundamental principles of governance and the 'direction of travel' for the New Direction administration not to repeat the mistakes of the discredited 'Orders from Above' status quo. This was often worsened by those Cabinet colleagues appointed by President Bio who demonstrated loyalty and committed support to the vice president and were often perceived to be in the vice president's political 'Camp'.

What the majority of the country do not seem to appreciate and understand is the simple fact that Vice President Dr. Mohamed Juldeh Jalloh is the most powerful vice president ever in the history of modern Sierra Leone. To the astute leadership credit of the vice president, given his loyalty and competence, coupled with the frequent travels of President Bio, all have virtually placed Vice President Juldeh Jalloh at the centre of governance in the New Direction administration with enormous and significant practical political, economic, and financial powers and authority in the country.

Managing Political Governance Relationships: The President, Vice President, Colleague Ministers, and the SLPP Leadership and Grassroots

In delivering the roles and mandate of the Chief Minister as assigned by or delegated by the President, the chief minister had to astutely and delicately manage and navigate several important governance-related and political relationships, including the principal relationship with the President as the 'Supreme Executive Authority'; the Vice President as 'Principal Assistant' to the President in the discharge of his Executive Functions[117]; colleague Ministers appointed by the President; and the SLPP leadership and grassroots.

No relationship is immune to the pressures of governance. In the course of our duties, there were bound to be instances of difficulty—tensions that are often the byproduct of deep commitment to a complex national agenda. Often the relational constraint may emerge in good faith about differences in personality and temperament, managing expectations, governance principles, and direction in the government

[117] Section 54 of the 1991 Constitution of Sierra Leone

focus and priorities. In the case of the chief minister and in hindsight, the difficult governance relationships were often heightened by the deliberate effort by some within the New Direction administration and the crude Machiavellian politics of 'Blaming Everything on Chief Minister'.

In terms of managing the governance relationship with the President as the 'Principal and Master', in the performance of my duties and responsibilities assigned or delegated, President Bio provided, on a consistent basis, 100 per cent high-level support and approval. However, there were areas where the president, for expedient political reasons and considerations, would withhold, in good faith, his presidential approval and might sometimes come across as 'throwing the chief minister under the Bus'.

In the execution of my diverse, complex and numerous functions, I never took these instances as an attempt to damage or destroy, the otherwise, very good working relationship between the President and the Chief Minister. I simply understood and accepted these moments as part and parcel of the role of Chief Minister, akin to taking the 'bullet for the Boss'. As Chief minister, I clearly understood that my role was to make the president and presidency look good with a credible national and international reputation as well as to make sure the government avoided or prevented any damaging scandal or distraction from the primary focus of delivering the government's agenda. This responsibility also went with the difficult task of always dispassionately informing the President and bringing bad news to the President on governance-related matters. Consistently, I prioritised the success of the New Direction administration over the comfort of a more convenient narrative. The challenge, in Mahatma Ghandi's words, was how do you 'Speak Truth to Power', to your 'Principal/Master' that has appointed you or assigned and delegated responsibilities to you. The one area in my governance relationship with President Bio that I have no regrets about, irrespective of the consequences, was my determination to always bring to his knowledge, in a respectful, cordial, and diplomatic way, the 'bad news' that everyone in governance was afraid to tell the President.

To successfully serve as chief minister and deliver in the role, the post holder must have the high-level trust, confidence, and respect of the President. The Chief Minister only functions because the President assigns and delegates responsibilities to the Chief Minister. The

President can, without notice, virtually make the Chief Minister redundant or 'useless' by withholding or refusing to assign or delegate any meaningful responsibilities.

With this strategic governance awareness, I came to the post of chief minister with the astute awareness that President Bio had spent most of his life in Sierra Leone and built long-standing, powerful political, socio-economic, and financial relationships and networks within the country and across the political divide. I came to realise that a professional, technocratic, and non-interest-based approach to governance and critical governance issues did not often sit well with the long-standing 'friends and close allies' of the president. Some of my chief minister governance interventions often put the President in a dilemma as to whether to go with the 'status quo' of business as usual or the New Direction mantra of effective political and economic management of the state.[118]

To underscore this point, the Sierra Eye magazine[119] publication on thc role of Chief Minister as Prime Minister, written by the eminent legal luminary and former senior APC Minister, Dr. Abdulia Conteh, was a damaging publication, deliberately slanted to imply that the Chief Minister, Professor David Francis, as 'Prime Minister', was more powerful in governance than President Bio, and if anything, it was the chief minister that was actually running the affairs of the state. The article, with its prominent front-page cover of pictures of the president and chief minister, questioned with the exaggerated headlines, 'President Bio Leading But Not in Charge?'. The posters/billboards advertising this particular SierraEye publication were strategically placed on the route that the president's convoy used on his way to the state house. In effect, making sure that the President sees this picture every day as he goes to work, which questioned whether, in fact, he was in control of governing the state. This particular publication was more than mere political mischief but a deliberate effort to instigate what Robert Greene, in the *48 Laws of Power*, described as the insecurity of the president and in the process, damaged our trusted and amicable working relationship. I must confess that after this publication, I noticed a thaw in our

[118] 'Effective political and economic management of the state' is a phrase borrowed from my book, 'Uniting Africa: building Regional Security Systems, Ashgate, 2006.
[119] SierraEye, 'Pres. Bio Leading But Not in Charge?', March – May 2020, Vol. 40.

relationship and distancing of the president from our otherwise close, amicable, and positive governance working relationship.

The governance relationship with the vice president and colleague ministers was mostly cordial and professional, despite the media-generated controversies and distractions that often attempted to portray the chief minister as usurping the role and functions of the constitutional vice president or as an unnecessary duplication of roles. This book has demonstrated with facts and evidence that the roles and functions assigned by or delegated by the president to the chief minister never conflicted with the role and mandate of the Vice President.

The governance relationship with colleague ministers was on the whole professional and positive, except for those who assumed that because of their close relationship and long friendship with the president, they were above supervision and performance management. I developed a professional, respectful, and disciplined working relationship with colleagues, publicly commending the effective management and performance of their respective ministries, and in some cases, stepping in to protect and defend colleague ministers who had made genuine mistakes or errors of judgement in carrying out their ministerial responsibilities.

As Chief Minister, I spent a lot of time on official field visits to colleague ministers in their respective ministries to have first-hand experience of the physical condition and state of affairs of their ministries and to listen to them and their senior staff on how to support them to effectively deliver services to the people. These official field visits were very useful because I reported back to the President the particular problems and challenges faced by respective ministries and what support the Presidency could provide to enable effective service delivery. Listening to colleagues, even those who had difficulties with my role, and taking a consistently proactive inclusive governance relationship all considerably helped to progress our high-performing team spirit and the collegial respect needed to work together and deliver on the President's agenda.

Perhaps the most challenging but rewarding relationship was that of managing the interface of the role of Chief Minister with that of the SLPP leadership and grassroots. To be clear, I assumed the role as Chief Minister with a very clear appreciation that the New Direction Government was only in power and governance because of the political party support of the people. In simple terms, without the grassroots support, the New Direction administration will not be running the affairs of the country at State House.

However, this created a particular challenge in terms of how to demarcate party politics from state governance issues, if that was ever possible. In the first four months of the New Direction administration, State House was often crowded with party supporters who had legitimately sacrificed so much to bring SLPP to power and elect President Bio. The President and State House were often inundated by party leadership and large groups of grassroots supporters, who would come to State House requesting job appointments, financial support for school fees, medical treatment, paying of house rents, student scholarships, Hajj pilgrimage, and all manner of requests that had nothing to do with state governance. I recognised that for the grassroots, political power is synonymous with patronage. In a landscape of scarcity, holding office is perceived as the fastest means of securing the distributive support necessary to mitigate the harsh 'bread and butter' realities facing the average citizen.

As such, this had an immediate impact on the ability of the president and State House officials to focus on and deliberate important nationwide governance delivery matters. I therefore recommended to President Bio to spend one day of each month, 12:00 – 6:00pm, at the Party HQs to engage with the SLPP leadership, meet with the party grassroots from across the country, and respond to their multiple problems. The 'Presidency – Party Interface Monthly Meeting' emerged as a cornerstone of our political strategy. This initiative was embraced and expertly coordinated by the party leadership—most notably the National Chairman, the National Secretary General, and the National Publicity Secretary—ensuring a seamless alignment between the administration's policy goals and the party's grassroots agenda.

However, and as always, we do not have the capacity to sustain the implementation of a good governance practice and culture, so the innovative monthly interface between the presidency and the party leadership and grassroots just fizzled out after three months. With the benefit of hindsight, and though this monthly presidential interface with the party grassroots was innovative and positively applauded, I realise it was one of my well-intentioned technocratic governance 'gimmicks' that I assumed would free up the president's most important resource, i.e., time, and at the same time, establish a new governance practice and culture.

On the whole, as chief minister, I had a positive relationship with the party leadership and grassroots, in particular, the party executive leadership, who individually and collectively supported my role and party-related activities as Chief Minister. Rejecting the tropes of traditional political rhetoric, I avoided the trap of making unrealistic promises to the grassroots. I believed that sustainable governance required a departure from the history of unfulfilled expectations, and I prioritised my credibility over the short-term gains of populist appeal. I supported all the key national party activities and grassroots projects. As Chief Minister, I deliberately avoided the political temptation to use the role and gravitas for politicking or to raise my national political profile and stature. Apart from my narrow development interventions in Kenema, I never did political tours on my own behalf to other districts in the Eastern region, such as Kailahun and Kono. Again and again, I had to remind myself that the role of the Chief Minister was that of a technocratic mandate and that the President never assigned or delegated political campaigning roles and responsibilities, aside from the explicit approval and directive from President Bio to lead on peace reconciliation and the development of Kenema.

Nevertheless, there was a rather small but misguided faction within the party elites that deliberately, and for political reasons, misinformed the grassroots and painted the negative picture and myth that I was alien to the party. They often sarcastically told the party grassroots supporters that the chief minister 'Na Jus kam. E nor bin dae na Saloneɛn SLPP'/'Just came back to Sierra Leone and SLPP'. This is and was simply not true! Surprisingly, nearly 90% of this rather misguided political party elite group were aware of my significant support and contribution to the SLPP dating back to 1996 and beyond. Most of them knew and interacted with me during my development support for President Ahmed Tejan Kabbah's government between 1996 and 2007 and my close professional and personal relationship with President Kabbah. They knew that I facilitated the award of an honorary doctorate to President Kabbah in 2006 at the University of Bradford in the UK and even wrote the 'Foreword' to his memoir published in 2010 entitled

Coming Back from the Brink in Sierra Leone: A Memoir.[120] This same politically motivated elite group knew that when vice president and SLPP Flag Bearer Rt. Hon. Solomon Berewa lost the 2007 presidential election, I invited him to the Department of Peace Studies, University of Bradford, as a resident - senior visiting research fellow for three months. I intellectually supported Solomon Berewa to write his memoir, which he published in 2011, entitled *A New Perspective on Governance, Leadership, and Nation Building in Sierra Leone.*[121] Additionally, this same group was well aware of the fact that when the SLPP presidential candidate, Julius Maada Bio, lost the 2012 presidential elections, I facilitated his admission to the University of Bradford and served as his PhD supervisor between 2014 and 2017. With all this formidable support to and for the SLPP, this politically motivated group determinedly portrayed me to the grassroots as 'Jus kam'/'New Arrival' to the party. The salient point that I am making is the fact that despite the deliberate efforts to plant a wedge between me as Chief Minister and the grassroots supporters, I have had a long and formidable relationship with the party. The motivation of this misguided elite group was obvious and sometimes negatively impacted my governance delivery role as Chief Minister.

Do We Need a Chief Minister?: The Scourge of Leadership Failure

The simple answer is yes and no. To critically address this rather difficult question, it is important to provide a broader intellectual and policy-practice context. Let me reiterate that the primary mandate of the chief minister as an innovative governance structure appointed by President Bio was to support, facilitate, and ensure the effective political and economic management of state affairs, to keep the New Direction administration focused on its agenda, and to deliver services with tangible benefits that impact the lives of the people across the country. In effect, the governance structure as symbolised in the Chief Minister was essentially about how to support the running of a country.

---

120 Ahmed TejanKabbah, Coming Back from the Brink in Sierra Leone: A Memoir, EPP Book Services, 2010

121 Solomon E. Berewa, A New Perspective on Governance, Leadership, Conflict and Nation Building in Sierra Leone, AuthorHouse UK, 2011.

This raises the academic and policy-relevant debate as to whether introducing or establishing a new governance structure will lead to effective management of the country and bring about the much-needed change in the lives of people in a poor country like Sierra Leone. The crucial question is, is it about re-creating governance structure, inclusive state governing institutions, or leadership or leadership failure and negative political culture? Juxtaposing the United States of America with Mexico, Daron Acemoglu and James Robinson, in *Why Nations Fail*[122], argue that inclusive institutions that are effective and based on accountable governance account for the success and failure of countries. Francis Fukuyama in *Political Order and Political Decay*[123] contends that the rule of law and accountable government are the prerequisites for the failure and success of states. Lew Kuan Yew in *From Third World to First*[124] persuasively tells the impressive story of how progressive, enlightened, and strong leadership made it possible for the successful nation building and state transformation of Singapore from a fishing village to a first-world country.

What can we then say about the governance context of Sierra Leone, and, in particular, how do we account for the prevailing status of the country as a poor and underdeveloped nation, despite its abundant natural and strategic mineral resources? Is re-creating the governance structure of the chief minister to make government work and deliver for the people simply enough? When it comes to the context of Sierra Leone and whether in fact we need a Chief Minister, we have to understand and appreciate the important fact that the Chief Minister governance structure operated within a context, i.e., the entrenched and negative, extractive, rent-seeking, nepotistic, and neo-patrimonial nature of domestic politics and 'shadow state' political culture. Therefore, no level of implementation of inclusive institutions as advocated by Acemoglu and Robinson, nor the prioritisation of the rule of law and accountable government as argued by Fukuyama, can be successful in the context of the 'Shadow State' domestic politics and political culture in Sierra Leone.

122 Daron Acemoglu & James Robinson, 'Why Nations Fail: the origins of power, prosperity and poverty' Profile Books, London, 2012

123 Francis Fukuyama, 'Political Order and Political Decay: From the Industrial Revolution to the Globalization of Democracy', Profile Books, London, 2014

124 Lee Kuan Yew, 'From Third World to First: Singapore and the Asian Economic Boom', HarperCollins, 2000

The simple reason is that the leadership or the small ruling and governing elites in control of state power are the very ones that use the negative political culture to subvert, privatise, informalise, and even turn state governing institutions into 'private market enterprises' for their selfish resource extraction, accumulation, and enrichment. State governing institutions, the rule of law, and accountable government sometimes do not work in the context of Sierra Leone, as in other modern liberal progressive countries, because the leaders, i.e., those political and economic elites in control of shadow state power, make the institutions what they are. In effect, the scourge of leadership failure has been the bane of Sierra Leone's underdevelopment and why the resource-rich country is consistently classified as poor and underdeveloped. Given these brutal political realities, questioning the need for a Chief Minister governance structure is no longer just a matter of theory. The complexities of our domestic landscape demand a central coordinating node, making the existence of such an office not an option, but a functional imperative for any transformative governance agenda.

Let me apply this context to my tenure in government as Chief Minister. The public perception in some quarters of the populace often portrayed the chief minister as a 'bad person' because of the strict, assertive leadership approach as well as my consistently professional, disciplined, and competent approach to governance. I came to governance with a very clear knowledge and expectation of how a government should and must run as an efficient political and economic system for the benefit of the people; at least, this is what I saw, experienced, and lived with in the UK, Europe, and America. Sadly, most citizens were not used to this type of professional and technocratic governance approach, devoid of the prevailing status quo 'PadiPadi (informal friendship) Governance Mentality and Culture', especially those political elites and their supporters who saw the attainment of political power as the primary means to access state resources to enrich themselves, their families, cronies, political party, and party stalwarts through the informal process of 'primitive accumulation'. The rather negative rent-seeking jibe often thrown at me as chief minister was *'Nor kam Spoil Ya'* (Do not dare to change or upset the status quo) that everyone was benefiting from.

My governance approach as chief minister, in support of President Bio, was to begin the difficult and challenging process of bringing genuine systemic change to make change happen and the socio-political reform needed to better the lives of the people. As Chief Minister, I genuinely believed in the imperative for change because Sierra Leone deserved better and had no reason to be a poor country, constantly described as an underdeveloped nation, despite its abundant natural, human, and strategic mineral resources.

With the benefit of hindsight, I now realise, though without regret, that though all the citizens talk about and want CHANGE, they are not, in particular, the small ruling and governing elites who find themselves in all the political parties, do not want change, and will go to extraordinary lengths to resist change and maintain the status quo that benefited them, whilst spurring out the rhetoric of 'Change of the Status Quo'.

As Chief Minister, I witnessed firsthand the negative attempt to fight back against any positive socio-political change that undermined the embedded 'particularist and sectional interests' of the political and economic elites, even though the change is designed to directly benefit the people and transform their lives for the better. It must be noted, however, that this resistance to transformative change is not unique to any one side of the political divide. This 'fight back' against positive socio-political reform is a systemic reality that confronts any political party assuming the leadership of the country; it is the natural reflex of a status quo that perceives progress as a threat to its survival. In fact, the context of Sierra Leone is not unique and applies to other countries in Africa as well.

Given the corrosive and devastating impact of the entrenched neo-patrimonial nature of domestic politics and political culture, the unbridled poverty mentality, and recurrent leadership failure, Sierra Leone is destined to remain poor and underdeveloped for the next 50 years if, as a country and people, we do not make the audacious, committed, and sustained effort to change for meaningful, effective political and economic management of the state through competent, disciplined, people-centred, and professional leadership.

Building on this candid evaluation, I present two essential observations on the future of governance in Sierra Leone. These points address the structural and cultural shifts necessary for the nation to transcend its current political limitations. First, Sierra Leone, a fantastically rich and resource-endowed country, is poor and underdeveloped because of the perpetual scourge of leadership failure. The politicians, the predatory ruling and governing elites or class, and, importantly, the people themselves are all responsible for the poverty-ridden and underdeveloped plight of Sierra Leone today! Second, even the few well-meaning, patriotic, technocratic, competent, professional, and disciplined national leaders that emerge in the context of the nature of domestic politics and the negative political culture often find themselves in the peculiar situation akin to what E. Edwards Deming aptly described as 'A bad system will beat a good person every time'. [125] In effect, this is not an Afro-pessimist conclusion about the future of the country but rather a realistic Afro-pragmatist reflection of the realities of contemporary Sierra Leone.

What Does this Book Say about Governance in Sierra Leone and Africa?

This authoritative book is about governance, governance reform and practice in the context of neo-patrimonial politics, political leadership, the resilience of post-war state building and development reconstruction, and institutional change in Africa, through the prism of Sierra Leone. *Governing a Poor Country* provides a refreshingly bold, frank, and audacious 'insider' critical perspective on the nature of governance in post-war Sierra Leone. Bearing in mind, state governance, in its simplest terms, is about running, managing, and administering state affairs as it pertains to public service delivery, socio-development management, economic development and stability, lawmaking and enforcement, and resource allocation. Across Africa and, in particular, Sierra Leone, state governance has been a challenge and part of the reason responsible for state failure and collapse, and in some extreme cases, has instigated violent conflicts and wars.

Therefore, this book attempts to ignite a public debate in Sierra Leone as to why the country suffers from perennial governance failures.

---

[125] Quoted by E. Edwards Deming, 26th February 2015, The Deming Institute, Phoenix, Arizona. Deming is of the view that a bad system (sic…*destructive political culture*) bears equal blame for failures as well as blaming leaders and people for any failure.

The perceptive accounts in this book have shown how those elected by the people with the mandate to change and transform the negative and unprogressive status quo and to reform and modernise state governing institutions and the political system, are faced with the difficult problem of how to cope with the 'fight back' and resistance to change and the reform agenda.[126] A critical insight from my tenure is the paradox of co-optation. We must recognise how easily reformers and change-makers can be integrated and co-opted into an extractive political system, where the pressures of neo-patrimonialism often neutralise the drive for genuine, people-centered service delivery.

The book presents the practice of governing a country and governance reform in a post-war fragile political environment not as a straightforward, sequential, or merely technical process. Practical governance has taught me that reform is neither linear nor deterministic, contrary to much of the established literature. The persistent failure of governance reforms across the continent can be explained by this gap: we are applying rigid, theoretical models to a fluid and resistant political environment that requires a much more adaptive approach.[127] State governance reforms are fundamentally shaped and influenced by improvisation, competition, managing diverse and often competing interests, coping with the tensions between national policy ambitions and local political realities, managing the expectations of what citizens expect and what the government can deliver, with the reform agenda driven by a rather dynamic and often at fast-moving pace. The important question is how can governance deliver for the people and achieve and sustain meaningful reform in the context of and against the background of the embedded socio-political and economic networks, interests, and loyalties that are inherently socio-political endeavours often detached from the needs and aspirations of the people, and the impact of the post-war institutional legacies.

As this book has factually illustrated, the simple and benign creation of national governance institutions such as NDMA and ICPNC were

---

[126] Ngozi Okonjo-Iweala, Fighting Corruption is Dangerous, MIT Press, 2018

[127] D. Dollar; S. Devaraya& T. Holmgren, 'Aid and Reform in Africa: lessons from Ten Case Studies, World Bank Publication, 2013; ESID Briefing, 'Public Sector Reform in Africa: understanding the paths and politics of change', No. 28, December 2017

not spared from the embedded neo-patrimonial interests and the patron – clientelistic loyalties. This is why I cautioned that rather than the self-serving and triumphant celebration of leading the establishment of these two state institutions, their creation should be seen as the beginning of a process of genuine reform that required negotiated mandates, fiscal stability, skilled and professional personnel, public legitimacy, and the ability of these newly created institutions to fully integrate into the broader national governance ecosystem.

The methodological framework has been a reflective approach, highlighting the problems and challenges of writing or giving an account of stewardship as both a participant/key player and as an 'objective' analyst. I have stated from the onset that this is not a purely academic and theoretical book, but a policy-practice critical reflection and documentation. I have provided a rather 'light-touch' theoretical framework and conceptual underpinning of the political economy analysis in the context of Sierra Leone to explain and foreground the nature of domestic politics and political culture based on prebendal politics and the neo-patrimonial state in Africa. For those academics, analyst, and policy practitioners who desire to further understand and appreciate the theoretical framework for this book, I have referenced the academic and theoretical literature on the principal – agent models, Michael Lipsky's street – level bureaucracy, political settlement, and liberal peacebuilding in post-war transition societies.[128]

The empirical evidence and case presented in this book attempt to answer and even raise further critical governance questions as to what conditions enable the rise of a 'delivery state' within entrenched power and interest-driven political systems. It questions whether a centralised governance reform and service delivery hub, like the role of the Chief Minister and the Office of the Chief Minister, could drive systemic change without provoking political backlash or the wrath of the entrenched sectional and particularist interests that control the Shadow State in Sierra Leone. Importantly, how can government balance central

[128] Michael Lipsky, Street-level Bureaucracy: the dilemmas of the individual in public service, Russell Safe Foundation, 1980; Sean Gailmard, 'Accountability and Principal – Agent Theory' in The Oxford Handbook of Public Accountability, Oxford University Press,, 2014; B. Voorn et al, 'Multiple Principals, Multiple Problems: implications for Effective Governance and a Resource Agenda for Joint Service Delivery', Public Administration, Vol 97, No. 3, 2019, pp. 671 – 685.

coordination with local autonomy in the implementation of services for the people, for example, the fallout between the central government and the Freetown City Council in the implementation of the National Cleaning Day programme. These are all critical governance challenges faced by poor and underdeveloped countries in Africa and globally.

Statecraft and governance reform in the context of post-war Sierra Leone involve the dynamic and often contradictory interaction between the political sphere and the socio-economic systems. In such a context, to carry out any socio-economic and development reform requires political will, leadership, and the momentum for change. In the context of Sierra Leone and as Chief Minister, I realised that governance reform and service delivery for the people was a dynamic, non-technocratic, and non-linear process that was often pragmatic, negotiated, and improvised and continually learned from the reform agenda limitations, and at the same time reflecting the underlying human, institutional, and interest motivations or texture of governance, largely driven by contestations, painstaking and thankless coordination, and compromise that forms the bedrock of public administration in a post-war transition country like Sierra Leone, where civil servants have a 'state capture mentality'.[129]

The seminal contribution of this groundbreaking and compelling book is that it audaciously opens the national debate on governance and demands answers as to why Sierra Leone, a resource-rich country, is constantly described and labeled as poor and underdeveloped. The central conclusion is that building efficient political and economic management of the state that delivers for the people depends not simply on policies and governance structures like the re-creation of the role of Chief Minister, but importantly on effective and visionary leadership, building credible and legitimate socio-political and technocratic relationships, and shared purpose of the vision, dream, aspiration, desire, and commitment to change and transform modern Sierra Leone into a middle-income and liberal progressive state. I have set out on this

---

129 State Capture as part of the broader literature on political economy analysis of neo-patrimonilaism and prebendal politics, refers to the way and manner in which formal governance laws, procedures and government bureaucracy are subverted and manipulated by government officials, including Civil Servants, to serve their personal, sectional, party-political and particularlist resource-accumulation interests. See Cheryl Saunders & Katrina Malone, State Capture: How to Recognise and React to it, Constitutional Insight No, 10, 2022.

critically reflective governance exploration of Sierra Leone to understand and appreciate what it truly means to govern a poor and for a long time, badly managed country; to confront scarcity; manage expectations; reconcile competing interests; and build state governing institutions that serve the public good, despite the challenging conditions.

Bibliography

Ahmed TejanKabbah, Coming Back from the Brink in Sierra Leone: A Memoir, EPP Book Services, 2010

Antonio A. T. Junior et al, Unlocking the Socio-economic Advantages of Cannabis Sativa L Legalization in Africa Countries: an in-depth review, Global Journal of Agricultural Research, Vol. 11, (1), 2023, pp. 32-52

B. Voorn et al, 'Multiple Principals, Multiple Problems: implications for Effective Governance and a Resource Agenda for Joint Service Delivery', Public Administration, Vol 97, No. 3, 2019, pp. 671 – 685

Bank Publication, Washington DC; World Bank, 'Sierra Leone Country Economic Memorandum' June 2025, World Bank Publication, Washington DC

Basita Michael, 'Pres. Bio Leading But Not in Charge?' SierraEye, March – May 2020

C. Magbaily Fyfe, The History of Sierra Leone: A Concise Introduction, Evans Africa, 1981

Cheryl Saunders & Katrina Malone, State Capture: How to Recognise and React to it, Constitutional Insight No, 10, 2022.

Cheryl Saunders & Katrina Malone, State Capture: How to Recognise and React to it, Constitutional Insight No, 10, 2022.

Chief Minister Professor David Francis, Address at Cabinet Retreat, 22-23 June 2018

Chief Minister, Professor David Francis' Statement at the Official Launch of the NDMA at State House on 19th November 2020.

Christopher Fyfe, A Short History of Sierra Leone, OUP, 1962

CITES _ Sierra Leone: Compliance Status, August 2021; CITES, Biennial Report for Sierra Leone CITES Management Authority for the Period 2020 – 2021;

CITES, National Report, IUCN, 2020

D. Dollar; S. Devaraya & T. Holmgren, 'Aid and Reform in Africa: lessons from Ten Case Studies, World Bank Publication, 2013

Daron Acemoglu& James Robinson, 'Why Nations Fail: the origins of power, prosperity and poverty' Profile Books, London, 2012

David J. Francis (ed). Peace, Democracy & Development in Africa, Adonis & Abbey, 2016

David J. Francis et al (eds.) Peace, Democracy & Development in Africa, Adonis & Abbey, London, 2016

David J. Francis, 'China – Sierra Leone Relations: Friendship, Cooperation and Win-Win Diplomacy, 2024

David J. Francis, 'Uniting Africa: building Regional Security Systems, Ashgate, 2006.

David J. Francis, 'When War Ends: Building Peace in Divided Communities' Aldershot, Ashgate, 2012

David J. Francis, The Politics of Economic Regionalism: Sierra Leone in ECOWAS, Ashgate, 2001

ESID Briefing, 'Public Sector Reform in Africa: understanding the paths and politics of change', No. 28, December 2017

Francis Fukuyama, 'Political Order and Political Decay: From the Industrial Revolution to the Globalization of Democracy', Profile Books, London, 2014

GoSL, The Forestry (Amendment Act) Act 2022

Independent Commission for Peace and National Cohesion Act, 2021, Published in Sierra Leone Gazette 5 on 4 February 2021

Jean Francois Bayart, 'The State in Africa: the Politics of the Belly' Polity Press, 1993

Joe A. D. Alie, Sierra Leone Since Independence: History of a Postcolonial State New Edition 2015

Lee Kuan Yew, 'From Third World to First: Singapore and the Asian Economic Boom', HarperCollins, 2000

Michael Barber, 'How to Run a Government: So That Citizens Benefit & Taxpayers Don't Go Crazy', Penguin Books, 2015

Michael Lipsky, Street-level Bureaucracy: the dilemmas of the individual in public service, Russell Safe Foundation, 1980

National Disaster Management Agency Act 2020, singed 8th June 2020 by H.E. Dr. Julius Maada Bio, President of the Republic of Sierra Leone,

Ngozi Okonjo-Iweala, Fighting Corruption is Dangerous, MIT Press, 2018

Office of the President, Government of Sierra Leone, Report of the Governance Transition Team 2018

Office of the President, Letter from Secretary to the President, 9 May 2018

Office of the President, State House, Freetown, Sierra Leone, 'Oath of Office as Acting Minister of Foreign Affairs and International Cooperation', 28th June 2018

Office of the President, State House, Letter of Appointment from Secretary to the President, 9 May 2018

Parliamentary Debates (Hansard) Official Hansard Report First Meeting of the First Session of the Fifth Parliament of the Second Republic of Sierra Leone, Proceedings of the Sitting of the House Held Tuesday, 8th May 2018

Robert Greene, '48 Laws of Power' Profile Books, 1998

Sean Gailmard, 'Accountability and Principal – Agent Theory' in The Oxford Handbook of Public Accountability, Oxford University Press, 2014

Sierra Eye, 'Pres. Bio Leading But Not in Charge?', March – May 2020, Vol. 40.

Sierra Leone Government, The Constitution of Sierra Leone 1991, Government Printing Department

Sierra Leone Telegraph, 'Sierra Rutile Mining Operations Resumes as Workers Agree to Return to Work', 4 December 20

Sierra Leone Telegraph, Abdul Rashid Thomas, 'President Bio has signed Ministerial Performance Contract –now up to Ministers to deliver' 8th February 2019, www.thesierraleonetelegraph.com)

Solomon E. Berewa, A New Perspective on Governance, Leadership, Conflict and Nation Building in Sierra Leone, Author House UK, 2011.

State House Press Release on the UNDP funded Green Paper provided 'Update on the Establishment of an Independent Commission for Peace and National Cohesion, 22th November 2018

State House Press Secretary, '57th Independence Anniversary Address to the Nation by His Excellency President Julius Maada Bio, 27th April 2019, Saika Stevens National Stadium

State House Press Secretary, 'Address by His Excellency President Julius Maada Bio at the Medium-Term Evaluation of the New Direction Government' at the Bintumani Conference Centre, on 24th January 2020

State House Press Secretary, 'Keynote Address by H.E. Dr Julius Maada Bio, President of Sierra Leone at the National Consultative

Conference at the Bintumani International Conference Centre on 23 May 2019

State House Press Secretary, 'President Bio Commits to 2030 Education Goal for Girls', 18th April 2018

State House Press Secretary, 'State Opening of Parliament Address on 18th May 2018 by H.E. President Julius Maada Bio.

State House Press Secretary, 'Statement by Chief Minister, Professor David Francis, at the Bintumani III National Consultative Conference on 23 May 2019 at Bintumani International Conference Centre

State House Press Secretary, 'Update on the GTT Report: Next Steps', 9th July 2018

State House Press Secretary, Executive Order No 1. Freetown, 9th April 2018

State House Press Secretary, His President Bio's Address to the Cabinet Retreat on 22 June 2018

State House Press Secretary, Inaugural Address by His Excellency President Julius Maada Bio at Saika Stevens Stadium on 12th May 2018

Statement by DG – NDMA, Lt. Gen. Brima Bureh Sesay, on 19th November 2020

Statement by H.E. President Julius Maada Bio on 19th November 2020 at the Official Launch of the NDMA at State House

Statement by World Bank Country Manager, G. Martin, Sierra Leone Telegraph, 28th November 2020, 'World bank Support Sierra Leone's Disaster Emergency Preparedness and Response Plan'. www.sierraleonetelepgrahp

Tony Blair, 'On Leadership: Lessons for the 21st Century', Hutchinson & Heinemann, 2024,

UNDP 2025, 'Towards 2025 Human Development Report (HDR) / Sierra Leone', UNDP Publication, NY; World Bank, 'Sierra Leone: Country Climate and Development Report' Country June 2025

UNDP Human Development Index Report 2025, 'A Matter of Choice: People and Possibilities in the Age of AI', UNDP Publication 2025;

William Reno, 'Corruption and State Politics in Sierra Leone' Cambridge University Press, 1998

William Reno, Corruption and State Politics in Sierra Leone, Cambridge University Press, 1998.

William Reno, Warlord Politics and African States', Lynne Rienner, Boulder, 1999

Annex I

List of GoSL Chief Ministers

1. Dr. Milton Margai. SLPP Head of Government and Leader in the British Colonial Administration's Legislative Assembly: 1954 - 1958
2. Professor David J. Francis: New Direction SLPP Government of President Dr. Julius Maada Bio: 2018 - 2021
3. Mr Jacob JusuSaffa: 2021 – 2023
4. Dr David M. Sengeh: 2023 - ditto

Annex II

List of GoSL Ministries 2018 – 2023

1. Chief Minister
2. Ministry of the Defence
3. Ministry of Environment and Forestry
4. Ministry of Transport and Aviation
5. Ministry of Foreign Affairs and International Cooperation
6. Ministry of Fisheries and Marine Resources
7. Ministry of Lands, Housing, and Country Planning
8. Ministry of Trade and Industry
9. Ministry of Water Resources
10. Ministry of Basic and Senior Secondary School Education
11. Ministry of Technical and Higher Education
12. Ministry of Finance
13. Ministry of Mines and Mineral Resources
14. Ministry of Youth Affairs
15. Ministry of Energy
16. Ministry of Planning and Economic Development
17. Ministry of Information and Communication
18. Ministry of Local Government and Rural Development
19. Ministry of Labour and Public Works
20. Ministry of Internal Affairs
21. Ministry of Gender and Children's Affairs
22. Ministry of Social Welfare
23. Ministry of Political and Public Affairs
24. Ministry of Health and Sanitation
25. Ministry of Agriculture and Food Security
26. Ministry of Justice and Attorney General
27. Ministry of Sports
28. Ministry of Tourism and Cultural Affairs.

Annex III

List of GoSL Legislated Agencies and Institutions in the Office of the President: 2018 - 2023

1. Anti-Corruption Commission (ACC)
2. Office of National Security (ONS)
3. Political Party Registration Commission (PPRC)
4. National Protected Area Authority (NPAA)
5. National Public Procurement Authority (NPPA)
6. Environment Protection Agency (EPA)
7. National Commission for Social Action (NaCSA)
8. National Arms Commission (NAC)
9. National Drug Law Enforcement Agency (NDLEA)
10. National Monitoring and Evaluation Agency (NaMED)
11. Directorate for Science and Technology (DSTI)
12. Office of Presidential Infrastructural Initiative (OPII)
13. National Disaster Management Agency (NDMA)
14. Independent Commission for Peace and National Cohesion (ICPNC)

More Books from David J. Francis

The Politics of Economic Regionalism: Sierra Leone in ECOWAS
Dangers of Co-deployment: UN Cooperative Peacekeeping in Africa (Co-authored)
Civil Militia: Africa's Intractable Security Menace (Edited Book)
Nation-States and the Challenges of Regional Integration in West Africa: Sierra Leone (Edited Book)
Uniting Africa: Building Regional Peace and Security Systems
US Strategy in Africa: Terrorism and Security Challenge (Edited Book)
Policing in Africa (Edited Book)
Peace and Conflict in Africa (Edited Book & Translated into Arabic)
When War Ends: Building Peace in Divided Communities (Edited Book)
African Peace Militaries: War, Peace, and Democratic Governance (Edited Book)
Peace, Democracy, and Development in Africa (Edited Book)
China–Sierra Leone Relations: Friendship, Cooperation, and Win-Win Diplomacy (Edited Book)

Index

H

I

J

K

M

N

O

P

S

T

U

V

W

Y

Z

www.ingramcontent.com/pod-product-compliance
Ingram Content Group UK Ltd.
Pitfield, Milton Keynes, MK11 3LW, UK
UKHW040202170226
468105UK00002B/85

9 781913 976743